BEST OF

New York City

Ginger Adams Otis

Best of New York City
3rd edition – February 2005
First published – April 2000

Published by Lonely Planet Publications Pty Ltd
ABN 36 005 607 983

Australia Head Office, Locked Bag 1, Footscray, Vic 3011
        ☎ 03 8379 8000 fax 03 8379 8111
        ⌨ talk2us@lonelyplanet.com.au
USA   150 Linden St, Oakland, CA 94607
        ☎ 510 893 8555 toll free 800 275 8555
        fax 510 893 8572
        ⌨ info@lonelyplanet.com
UK   72–82 Rosebery Avenue, London EC1R 4RW
        ☎ 020 7841 9000 fax 020 7841 9001
        ⌨ go@lonelyplanet.co.uk

This title was commissioned in Lonely Planet's Oakland
office and produced by: **Commissioning Editor** Jay Cooke
Coordinating Editor Holly Alexander **Coordinating
Cartographer** Alison Lyall **Layout Designer** Sonya Brooke
Editors Lucy Monie, Jocelyn Harewood **Cartographers**
Lachlan Ross, Julie Sheridan, Csanad Csutoros, Amanda
Sierp **Managing Cartographer** Alison Lyall **Cover
Designer** Pepi Bluck, James Hardy **Project Manager**
Glenn van der Knijff **Mapping Development** Paul Piaia
Thanks to Chris LeeAck, Eoin Dunlevy, Fiona Siseman,
Laura Jane and Kerryn Burgess

Photographs by Lonely Planet Images and Dan Herrick
except for the following: p5, p7, p10, p18, p23, p24, p46,
p49, p50, p51, p52, p65, p87, p93, p102, p107, p108,
Angus Oborn/Lonely Planet Images, p21 John Banagan/
Lonely Planet Images, p21 Kim Grant/Lonely Planet
Images. **Cover photograph** Aerial view of cabs on New
York street, Michael N. Paras/PhotoLibrary.

All images are copyright of the photographers unless
otherwise indicated. Many of the images in this guide
are available for licensing from Lonely Planet Images:
  ⌨ www.lonelyplanetimages.com

ISBN 1 74104 124 4

Printed by Markono Print Media Pte Ltd, Singapore

Acknowledgements Grateful acknowledgment is made
for reproduction permission: New York City Subway Map
© 2004 Metropolitan Transportation Authority.

Lonely Planet and the Lonely Planet logo are trademarks
of Lonely Planet and are registered in the US Patent and
Trademark Office and in other countries.

Lonely Planet does not allow its name or logo to be
appropriated by commercial establishments, such as
retailers, restaurants or hotels. Please let us know of any
misuses: ⌨ www.lonelyplanet.com/ip

HOW TO USE THIS BOOK

Color-Coding & Maps

Each chapter has a color code along the
banner at the top of the page which is also
used for text and symbols on maps (eg all
venues reviewed in the Highlights chapter
are orange on the maps). The fold-out
maps inside the front and back covers are
numbered from 1 to 6. All sights and venues
in the text have map references; eg (3, C4)
means Map 3, grid reference C4. See p128
for map symbols.

Prices

Multiple prices listed with reviews (eg $10/5/2)
usually indicate adult/child/discount admission
to a venue. Discount prices can include senior,
student, member or coupon discounts. Meal
cost and room rate categories are listed at
the start of the Eating and Sleeping chapters,
respectively.

Text Symbols

☎   telephone
⊠   address
⌨   email/website address
$ admission
☸   opening hours
ⓘ   information
⊖   subway
🚌   bus
⚓   ferry/boat
♿   wheelchair access
✕   on-site/nearby eatery
♟   child-friendly venue
Ⓥ   good vegetarian selection

Contents

From the Publisher

AUTHOR

Ginger Adams Otis

Ginger Adams Otis moved to New York City in 1995, at the height of the city's housing boom. With $50 in her pocket and images of a Soho loft dancing in her head, she navigated the mean streets on a shoestring budget (sleeping on friend's couches), gradually building a career as a journalist and travel writer. Ginger has written for publications such as the *Village Voice,* the *Nation, Newsday, Ms Magazine, JANE,* the *Ex-Berliner* and *In These Times,* and also does radio work for Pacifica, the Associated Press, National Public Radio and the BBC. Although her assignments take her far and wide, Ginger is always happy to return home to her beloved NYC and (at last!) her Nolita apartment.

To the fabulous Jay Cooke in the LP Oakland office, thanks for the enthusiasm, the support, the feedback, the hours and effort you put into this project. Did I ever tell you how grateful I am for this opportunity, and for your guidance? I am forever in the debt of Holly in Australia, whose fine editorial eye saved me from many a gaffe, and greatly improved the finished product. To all the others in California and Australia who helped with maps and random questions, and to LP's previous NYC authors, a big thank you for the behind-the-scenes propping up! Last, but not least, thanks to my friends who stayed out 'til the wee hours and gave up weekends and weeknights to play tourist. Finally, thank you to the beautiful, inspiring, everchanging city of New York that has become my home.

The 1st and 2nd editions of this book were written by Dani Valent.

PHOTOGRAPHER

Dan Herrick

Dan Herrick has lived in New York City for four years. He completed work for the guide during a busy month between elections and Fashion Week. His favorite place to photograph was Coney Island – rich with all its interesting characters and history. At the end of the day his stomach hurt from all the hot dogs and cheese fries that he found on the boardwalk. Deciding that it would not be prudent to ride the Cyclone rollercoaster, he recovered on the beach and ended up making new friends. He could not resist playing a few booth games although he did not walk away with any stuffed animals. Like most busy New Yorkers he had never visited attractions such as the Statue of Liberty and the Cloisters; these he visited for the first time to photograph.

SEND US YOUR FEEDBACK

We love to hear from travelers – your comments keep us on our toes and help make our books better. Our well-traveled team reads every word on what you loved or loathed about this book. Although we cannot reply individually to postal submissions, we always guarantee that your feedback goes straight to the appropriate authors, in time for the next edition – and the most useful submissions are rewarded with a free book. To send us your updates – and find out about Lonely Planet events, newsletters and travel news – visit our award-winning website: 🖳 **www.lonelyplanet.com/feedback.**

Note: We may edit, reproduce and incorporate your comments in Lonely Planet products such as guidebooks, websites and digital products, so let us know if you don't want your comments reproduced or your name acknowledged. For a copy of our privacy policy visit 🖳 www.lonelyplanet.com/privacy.

Introducing New York City

Spend a few days in New York City and you'll feel like you've seen the world. Where else can you take the subway four stops and transport yourself from Little Korea to Little Italy? Or one moment be standing in teeming Midtown, surrounded by hustling New Yorkers intent on making their next buck, or that lunch date, or whatever business they've got going on, and next thing you know you're just south of Houston, where time is stuck somewhere between here and 1895 and people seemingly have nowhere special to go. New York is full of dynamic contrasts; weighted down by wall-to-wall buildings and more than eight million people, it's essentially a city of neighborhoods, each with its own unique flavor and pace.

Nowhere is the dynamism more apparent than in the people. New Yorkers eat kimchi and Korean BBQ, falafel, gyros, *pirzola* (Turkish ribs), and borscht. They dance salsa, merengue and bachata when the mood strikes, head to Little Brazil when they need a *futbol* (soccer) fix, and generally consider national and international politics as something that's happening in their own backyard. And that's not hubris talking – more foreign and domestic embassies, corporations, foundations and cultural institutions are headquartered here than anywhere else in the country (and that's not even counting the UN). It's up to you to take a deep breath and dive right in. First-rate ballet? World-class sports? Museum tours and pub crawls and all-night Lower East Side poetry slams? It's all there, and more. Mix and mingle, meet and greet, and – as the locals do – let it all hang out. How much can happen in a New York minute? Brace yourself – you're about to find out.

Central Park, Fifth Ave, Wall St – downtown delights

Neighborhoods

Go left, and there's Chinatown; right, and you're in Soho. Harlem is uptown, the Financial District is downtown, and Hell's Kitchen, Nolita, and the Loisada are all cool places to live. It may sound like an alphabet soup

Wall Street on a plate

of insider knowledge, but what it boils down to is that New Yorkers love to name their 'nabes' – those little pockets of culture and color that give the city its unique sense of place and style. Here's a basic breakdown of Manhattan, starting at the southern tip and heading north.

Wall St and **Battery Park** (aka **Lower Manhattan**, pp10–11) are filled with huge, hulking skyscrapers crammed into an area built on a colonial scale. It makes for some fascinating architecture and cityscapes, which is why the area has been dubbed 'the concrete canyon' by locals.

North of the Brooklyn Bridge, vibrant **Chinatown** (p14) explodes eastward along Canal St and into the **Lower East Side** (Loisada), all of which used to be known as **Little Italy**. That community is now basically confined to Mulberry St, where just a few remaining Italian-American families work hard to keep 'old country' traditions alive. Just north of Broome St but still below Houston St is **Nolita** (North of Little Italy), formerly a gritty area but now a bright and bubbly upscale quadrant of pretty city blocks.

To the west of Lafayette St, galleries, boutiques and the occasional cobblestone road give both **Soho** (South of Houston) and **Tribeca** (the Triangle Below Canal) a gentle fin-de-siècle feel. Nineteenth-century factories once filled this area, until artists began turning the derelict cast-iron buildings into soaring loft spaces in the sixties.

North of Houston St on Sixth Ave is **Greenwich Village** (p16), known more familiarly as 'the village.' It remains true to its 19th-century heritage as a haven for creative types, and is a great place to while away a sunny afternoon. On the east side below 14th St is the **East Village** (p15), once an edgy neighborhood of immigrants,

Live the soulful life in Harlem

raconteurs and anarchists and now home to clean-cut students and young executives. Above 14th St is **Union Sq**, a popular gathering spot at the nexus of several major subway and bus lines, surrounded by elegant hotels. It's also the southern gateway to **Gramercy Park** and the **Flatiron District**, a well-heeled section of townhouses and shops.

Heading west along 14th St to Ninth Ave will bring you to the **Meatpacking District**, which still houses several working abattoirs

Never tried Ukranian? Try Veselka (p77)

amidst its growing crop of hip hotels, eateries and nightclubs. This area overlaps with **Chelsea**, a neighborhood filled with art galleries and trendy cafés catering to the upper 20-year-olds.

Teeming **Midtown** (34th St to 59th St) holds many of the city's most popular attractions, including **Rockefeller Center** (p21), **Times Sq** (p20), the theater district and Grand Central Terminal. To the west is **Hell's Kitchen** (aka **Clinton**), the latest neighborhood to get a gentrifying face-lift that's brought in some high-end hotels and popular watering holes.

Across town is the **Upper East Side**, which contains the **Museum Mile** (p46) and **Fifth Avenue** (p22). The **Upper West Side** has quiet, tree-lined boulevards running parallel to **Central Park** (p25) all the way into **Morningside Heights** and **Harlem** (p27), home to gospel churches, jazz, plenty of good food with a decidedly international flavor and some of the most beautiful brownstones in Manhattan. **Spanish Harlem** tops off Park Ave above 110th St, and Columbia University students rub elbows with resonant immigrant communities in **Washington Heights** and **Inwood**, not far from Fort Tyron Park and the Cloisters.

Brooklyn and Beyond

Brooklyn is booming for good reason. **Park Slope**, the **Heights** and **Cobble Hill** are gorgeous, townhouse-filled neighborhoods with swanky bistros and working-class diners. **Williamsburg** is a postmodernist-meets-Polish blend of hipsters and Hasidim with a vibrant nightlife, and if you want to hit **Brighton Beach**, better brush up on your Russian. **Carroll Garden** and **Red Hook** are the two newest 'nabes' currently undergoing something of a cultural and foodie renaissance. Every New Yorker knows that there's some mouthwatering food to be had just over the East River, in Queens. **Long Island City**, **Astoria** and **Jackson Heights** offer a cutting-edge art scene, to-die-for-Greek food, and fantastic Indian eats, respectively.

Itineraries

Manhattan is easy to explore if you're going uptown or downtown – it's when you want to go crosstown that things get complicated! Most New Yorkers get by with a combination of subway, bus and foot transport (with the occasional cab thrown in) and your best bet is to do the same. The city is bursting with fabulous things to see and do, but don't forget that strolling is a big part of life in NYC – factor in time to saunter the streets.

When I grow up, I want to be a statue

Pick up a MetroCard (p114) from any newsstand or subway station and start planning; an efficient way to sightsee is to take a bus or subway train to an area you want to explore and then hoof it from sight to sight. When you're ready for a change, go to a totally different part of town and soak it up.

First Time

Head to Lower Manhattan to check out the Statue of Liberty and Ellis Island (or jump on the Staten Island Ferry for a quick drive-by look if lines are too long for the full tour). Have a bite at South St Seaport and inhale the briny atmosphere while waiting for the M15 bus to Chinatown. From there explore Tribeca, Soho and Little Italy. As dusk approaches get to the Empire State Building for sunset and then hit Times Sq for a neon-lit dinner (and maybe a show).

Uptown

Greet the morning from Riverside Park, then check out Cathedral of St John the Divine in Morningside Heights. From there, it's two steps to Harlem and a history lesson at Schomberg Center. Soul food awaits at Sylvia's, and don't forget the Apollo Theater, Striver's Row and the Studio Museum. A cup of java at Settepani's, and then hit the Museum Mile on the Upper East Side. Finish with a before-dinner stroll along Central Park.

Worst of New York City
NYC does have a few things that can work your nerves:
- MetroCards that won't swipe: happens all the time, but don't even think about jumping that turnstile – somebody *is* watching.
- Subway delays: that local train that suddenly became an express? Now it's out of service.
- Sidewalk smoking: it's everywhere, particularly at night when barflies light up outside.

Downtown

Breakfast in the West Village and then window-shop to Washington Sq Park. Move on to the East Village, following St Marks Pl into Tompkins Sq. Cross Houston St for a late lunch at Schiller's, gallery hopping on Rivington, drinks in Nolita, and then catch a cab to the Meatpacking District for some nightclubbing. Stave off midnight munchies at Florent.

Highlights

STATUE OF LIBERTY (4, A3)

Presented to the USA in 1886 as a gift from France, the Statue of Liberty, engraved with the words of Emma Lazarus ('Give me your tired, your poor,/ Your huddled masses yearning to breathe free'), has welcomed millions of immigrants to their new home and still inspires awe in all who behold it. *Liberty Enlightening the World* is the statue's official name, and it was sculpted by Frederic-Auguste Bartholdi (Gustav Eiffel designed the iron skeleton). It stands 305ft (93m) tall and weighs 225 tons. To just stroll around the statue you only need ferry tickets; to go inside you must make a 'Time Pass' reservation with the National Parks Service. The 'Time Pass' is good for one hour (you stipulate the hour you want, say 9am to 10am, and as long as you arrive at the statue before 10am, you'll be allowed in), offering

INFORMATION
- ☎ 212-363-3200; ferry info ☎ 212-269-5755; Time Passes ☎ 866-782-8834
- 📖 www.nps.gov/stli; Time Passes 📖 www.statuereservations.com
- ✉ Liberty Island
- 💲 statue free admission; ferry $10/4
- 🕐 9am-5pm (to 6:30pm Jun-Aug)
- ● Circle Line ferry departs Battery Park every 20-30min 8:30am-late afternoon, stops first at Liberty Island, then continues to Ellis Island
- ● 5 to Bowling Green; 1, 9 to South Ferry
- ♿ to base only
- 🍴 kiosk

DON'T MISS
Castle Clinton National Monument, built as a fort in 1807 in Battery Park, is a visitor center and ticket booth for ferries to Ellis Island and the Statue of Liberty. Look for **The Immigrants** near the entrance, a renowned sculpture by Luis Sanguino depicting strangers huddled together and drawing solace from each other as they wait hopefully for admittance to America.

two guided tour options (both are free). One tour goes through the promenade, into the statue's pedestal and then out to surrounding Fort Wood. The other tour includes a stop at the **Observatory Deck**, which is 24 steps above the museum and features entrancing views – almost as good as those from the crown (which is no longer open to the public).

The **museum** has great exhibits detailing Lady Liberty's history and the grounds, while small, are verdant and inviting on a sunny day. The ferries loop between this island, Ellis Island and Manhattan with spectacular views all the way. For the best photos, sit on the right going out and the left coming back. Be aware: lines for the ferry can be very long and security checks add more delays, so head out early and be prepared to wait. For good views without delays, take the Staten Island Ferry (free) or grab a New York Water Taxi (p114) for a drive-by experience.

LOWER MANHATTAN (3, C7–9 & D7–9)

An eye-catching combination of the old and the new, the southern tip of Manhattan contains some of the island's most grandiose skyscrapers crammed onto tiny colonial streets. This is where the city was

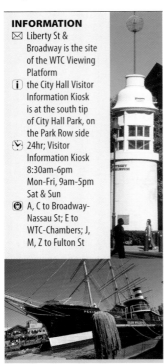

INFORMATION
- ✉ Liberty St & Broadway is the site of the WTC Viewing Platform
- ℹ the City Hall Visitor Information Kiosk is at the south tip of City Hall Park, on the Park Row side
- ⏲ 24hr; Visitor Information Kiosk 8:30am-6pm Mon-Fri, 9am-5pm Sat & Sun
- Ⓔ A, C to Broadway-Nassau St; E to WTC-Chambers; J, M, Z to Fulton St

Your ship's coming in at South St Seaport

born, first as a native Lenape settlement, then a Dutch colony, later a British stronghold and the (temporary) capital of a new and free nation. Lower Manhattan is overflowing with Revolutionary and modern landmarks: George Washington was sworn in as the first president at **Federal Hall National Memorial** (3, D8; p33) and slept at **Fraunces Tavern** (3, D8); the graveyards at **Trinity Church** (3, C8) and **St Paul's Chapel** (3, C7) are filled with founding fathers; the **African Burial Ground** (3, D7; p104) has emerged in recent years to tell a more complete story of New York's origins; and the **New York Stock Exchange** (3, C8; p34) continues to wield its massive financial influence across the far corners of the globe.

The World Trade Center (WTC) towers certainly added the most dramatic touch to the spiky skyline and their destruction in 2001 left a visible hole that has yet to be filled, but Lower Manhattan has quickly learned to focus on what can be regained rather than on what has been irrevocably lost. The **World Financial Center** (3, C8; p34), which was nearly blown apart that September day, has reopened its famed **Winter Garden** in a glass-enclosed atrium and continues to hold symposiums, concerts, recitals, art showings, exhibitions and competitions, as well as dance events and theatrical presentations. Stretching up the west side, **Battery Park** (3, C9; p36) has reinstalled its award-winning collection of public art, the **Statue of Liberty** (4, A3; p9) is once again available to the public, and across the way on the East River, marvelous **South St Seaport** (3, D8) has opened up a whole new building of galleries dedicated to maritime art. Opposite the Seaport, **Schermerhorn Row** (the first block in the country to receive electricity) faces quaint cobblestone streets adorned with renovated 19th-century buildings that house restaurants and shops.

Wall St (3, D8), running from Broadway to the East River, is the main artery of Manhattan's Financial District. It's one of the busiest and most visited parts of the city, drawing hundreds of thousands of workers every day. The whole area is reminiscent of a huge canyon, especially in early mornings when bright shafts of sunlight cut through the skyscraper tops and cast oddly-patterned shadows on the small, dark and crooked streets below. From the tip of **Bowling Green** (3, C9) one can see right up

Washington meets Medici at Federal Hall

the 'Canyon of Heroes,' site of many a ticker tape parade. Also in Bowling Green is '**Wall Street Bull**,' or '**Charging Bull**,' a 7,000lb (3175kg) bronze statue made by Italian-born artist Arturo Di Modica and illegally placed in front of the New York Stock Exchange in 1989. Di Modica decided to create the bull after Black Monday, October 19, 1987, the day of the largest 24-hour decline in recorded stock market history. The police were called in to haul the bull away but public outcry was such that the New York City Department of Parks and Recreation made room for it. Nearby is the **National Museum of the American Indian** (3, C8; p30) in the old **US Custom House**, the **Skyscraper Museum** (3, C8; p30) in Battery Park City, and one of Manhattan's least visited but most beautiful sights, the **Vietnam Veteran's Memorial** (3, D9) next to the water.

Ground Zero

The viewing platform has been removed and Ground Zero can now be seen from many perspectives, while on-site panels detail the history of the WTC, the tragic events of 9/11 and the heroic efforts of the recovery workers. However, the most intimate look comes on the PATH train ride in from New Jersey, which snakes through the remains of the concrete foundations. Beautiful banners extolling the virtues of New York have turned the station into a working memorial of sorts.

ELLIS ISLAND (4, A2)

From 1892 to 1954 more than 17 million people fleeing poverty, civil strife or religious unrest in their homelands entered America via this tiny island. As big steamships rolled into New York, first- and second-class passengers were processed on board and gently deposited on city docks; poor travelers from steerage class were unloaded onto Ellis Island, where they underwent medical and legal examinations. Frightened and exhausted, clutching papers, money and some family belongings, up to 5,000 people passed through in a day – and those were the lucky ones who weren't pulled aside for reasons that were often bewilderingly unclear to non-English speakers. In the **Registry Room (Great Hall)** officials weeded out 'undesirables,' which included unmarried women, the totally destitute and the mentally or physically infirm.

INFORMATION
- ☎ 363-3200, ferry info
  ☎ 269-5755
- 🖳 www.nps.gov/elis
- ✉ Ellis Island
- 💲 museum free admission; ferry $10/4
- 🕐 museum 9am-5pm (to 6:30pm Jun-Aug)
- ⓘ audio tour $6
- 🚢 Circle Line ferry departs Battery Park every 20-30min 8:30am to late afternoon, stops first at Liberty Island, then continues to Ellis Island
- Ⓢ 5 to Bowling Green; 1, 9 to South Ferry
- ♿ excellent
- 🍴 kiosk

Governors Island

For two centuries this 127-acre island half a mile from Manhattan has been under military control. It's now open for tours (in summer only, from June to September) and the seawall esplanade is great for picnicking. Tickets are sold at South St Seaport Museum; the ferry departs Battery Maritime Building at 10 South St.

More than 30 galleries of artifacts, photographs and taped oral histories bring the immigrant experience alive in a vivid and memorable way. The visitors desk has tickets to a free film that highlights the often heartbreaking effort it took for immigrants to leave home, as well as information on the ranger tour times and special programs. For history buffs, the ranger tours are well worth the wait. At a computer terminal at the **American Family Immigration Center** you can (for a fee) search Ellis Island's records for your own ancestors. It's amazing to think that fully 40% of the USA's population descends from someone who passed through these doors.

BROOKLYN BRIDGE (3, E7–8)

For a superlative city experience, walk or bike across the Brooklyn Bridge on a fine day and drink in the exhilarating expanse of space that opens up around you. The bookend views of tightly squeezed Manhattan and busy Brooklyn are all the more enjoyable when taken in from such a lofty perch. This superbly graceful structure, the first steel suspension bridge ever built, was considered an engineering marvel in 1883 when it opened to the public. Early rumors that the bridge was unsound weren't helped by the fact that 20 workers were killed building it,

INFORMATION
- ✉ pedestrian entrance on Park Row
- ⏱ 24hrs
- Ⓜ 4, 5, 6 to Brooklyn Bridge-City Hall
- ✖ Brooklyn: River Café (see p80)

DON'T MISS VIEWS
- waiting-to-be developed Governors Island in the middle of the harbor
- the Verrazano-Narrows Bridge looming in the distance
- South St Seaport's busy docks crammed with tall ships
- Lady Liberty's gaze – right into Brooklyn (she's really looking sternly at Europe, which the sculptor felt was 'unenlightened' at the time)

including designer John Roebling, who died of gangrene shortly after a meandering ferryboat rammed his foot while he was at work on a pier. His son took over the project but (like so many workers) got the bends during the underwater excavation period and was permanently crippled. Thereafter he supervised operations from a telescope in his sick room. To top it off, 12 pedestrians were trampled when the crowd mistakenly thought the bridge was collapsing during the inaugural ceremony and broke into a panicked run.

It takes about 20 minutes to cross the 1 mile (1.8km) expanse. There are designated lanes on the bridge to avoid collisions – foot traffic to the north side, bicyclists to the south – but pedestrians still need to keep a sharp eye out for bicyclists and in-line skaters, as those traveling on wheels tend to zip right along. The views are mesmerizing, particularly between the twin Gothic arches.

CHINATOWN & LITTLE ITALY (3, D6–7 & E6–7)

A living example of how immigrant communities arrive, thrive and move on in New York: what was once Little Italy is now almost entirely Chinatown, save for one or two small blocks right above Canal St. Regardless of which ethnicity calls the neighborhood home, it's a vibrant and exotic location. Roughly half of its residents speak little or no English and there's a constant overlapping of festivals, holidays and traditions. Home to a whopping 200 restaurants and bars, this is a place New Yorkers favor when they really want to let loose and live a little (karaoke, anyone?).

INFORMATION

✉ Canal St and W Broadway bounded by Houston St to the north and flowing east into Delancey St

☎ New York Chinatown Visitor's Center
    ☎ 212-274-8880

▣ www.chinatown search.com; www. chinatownnyc.com

◉ J, M, Z, N, R, 6 to Canal St

♿ fair

Bloody Angle
Early Chinese immigrants were mostly young men who sometimes joined *tongs* (gangs). In the 1920s, so many gang-related killings occurred at the sharp curve in Doyer St that it became known as the 'Bloody Angle.' No longer the dangerous hangout it once was, Doyer St now has several excellent vegetarian restaurants.

The city's layered immigrant history is evident everywhere, particularly at the **Church of the Transfiguration** (3, D6), the focal point of the Chinese Roman Catholic Community. Nearby the **Eastern States Buddhist Temple** (3, D6) has 100 gold Buddhas gleaming in candlelight. On the Bowery, contemporary art is displayed at the **Asian American Arts Centre** (3, D6). The **Museum of Chinese in the Americas** (3, D6) features a fascinating exhibit called 'Where is Home?' and tons of kitschy kiosks selling knock-offs and knick-knacks line Canal St. Pedestrian-only **Mott** and **Mulberry Sts** specialize in alfresco dining, and all along the edge of Chinatown, even as it pushes into the Lower East Side, small Vietnamese, Japanese, Malaysian and Taiwanese shops and eateries have begun to appear, adding even more depth to this dizzying cultural experience.

EAST VILLAGE   (3, D4–5, E4–5, F4–5)

Gritty tenement dwellings line these piquant streets and the area's abundant creative energy makes this a popular and upbeat neighborhood. Locals may bemoan the gradual erosion of immigrant and working-class culture, but enough rough edges still exist to keep the East Village completely authentic, and always interesting.

Remnants from previous inhabitants abound, particularly above Houston St, where the counter-culture movement that took over the East Village during the 1960s – think Jack Kerouac, Allen Ginsberg, the Electric Circus – clings to its turf, mixing freely with the latest wave of young financiers and recent grads. Artists-in-residence hang at **St Mark's-in-the-Bowery Church** (3, D4), pink-haired punks and dark-eyed goths (along with tattoo- and piercing-seekers) still converge at **Tompkins Sq Park** (3, E4) and **St Mark's Place** (3, E4) but most evenings it's all about the club crawl – streets are jammed with limos, taxis and highly energized pedestrians, all wanting a piece of this 'nabe.' Even the once-sketchy Alphabet City (named for avenues A, B, C and D) now has stylish and high-end restaurants. *The Cube,* an abstract sculpture on a traffic island at **Astor Pl** (3, D4) serves as the unofficial entrance to the East Village (and it spins if you push it hard enough), and Second Ave's heterogeneous blend of Indian, Ukrainian and hipster cultures – seen best at **St George's Ukrainian Catholic Church** (3, D4), a knockout with three brightly colored murals – makes it a striking and stimulating street.

INFORMATION

✉ btwn 14th St to the north, Broadway to the west, Houston St to the south and the East River

🚇 6 to Astor Pl

♿ fine

Ave C: it's hair-raising

The Lower East Side

Get a taste of early immigrant life with a visit below Houston St east of the Bowery. In the 1920s refugees mostly from Eastern Europe turned this into one of the world's most densely populated areas; entire families lived in one-room apartments and slaved in unregulated clothing factories (today we call them sweatshops). The **Lower East Side Tenement Museum** (3, E5; p29) on Orchard St conducts guided tours through an old immigrant residence – make sure to stop at **Guss Pickles** (3, E6; 85-87 Orchard St; ☾ 9.30am-6pm Sun-Thu, 9.30-sunset Fri) on Orchard St.

GREENWICH VILLAGE (3, B4–5, C4–5, D4–5)

Made up of old cow paths that double back on each other and hidden courtyards that peek from behind narrow, tree-lined alleys, the 'Village' is still reminiscent of the far-flung rural outpost it once was,

INFORMATION
- ✉ btwn 14th St to the north, Broadway to the east, Houston St to the south and the Hudson River
- Ⓜ 1, 9 to Christopher St-Sheridan Sq
- ♿ fine

Under the arch of Washington Sq Park

when wealthy New Yorkers fled Lower Manhattan's smallpox epidemics in the 1800s. Even when the city grew well beyond 14th St, residents never ceded the lovely country atmosphere they'd grown accustomed to. In 1831 **New York University** broke ground in nearby **Washington Sq** (3, C4) and a new crowd began to move in; the university's fiery politics and liberal attitudes attracted growing numbers of artists and activists, as well as a large gay and lesbian community. The neighborhood's bohemian roots began to take hold.

Not Your Average Village Idiots

- Eugene O'Neill and ee cummings lived at Patchin Pl on W 10th St.
- Once a Prohibition-era speakeasy, Chumley's (p000) hosted Faulkner, Steinbeck and Hemingway.
- The Stonewall Riot, birth of the gay rights movement, occurred here in 1969.
- Jack Kerouac, Allen Ginsberg and William Burroughs met at Mac-Dougal and Bleecker for coffee.

Plenty of literary lights from multiple generations got turned on in the Village. Early American writers Edith Wharton, Mark Twain and Henry James lived and worked opposite **Washington Sq Park**; Willa Cather wrote six novels at **5 Bank Street** (3, B4) and Welsh poet Dylan Thomas drank himself to death one night in the **White Horse Tavern** (p44): James Baldwin dropped in and out of Village life between jaunts back up town to Harlem and Bob Dylan sang his first folk song at the Washington Sq fountain. Abstract expressionists like de Kooning congregated on street corners and Jack Kerouac and the Beat Generation came of age on **Bleecker St** (3, B4). Still home to lots of New York artists and freethinkers, today's Village has been scrubbed clean of its most colorful dives, although plenty of funky cabaret and blues bars keep the crowds coming.

UNION SQUARE GREENMARKET (3, C3)

Fresh corn, tomatoes, zucchini and flowers are as easy to get in the city as in 'the country' (anyplace outside the 212 area code for New Yorkers), thanks to the fabulous open-air farmers' markets, known as greenmarkets, held in all five boroughs. Founded in 1976, greenmarkets provide an opportunity for regional growers to sell fresh farm products directly to residents, while greenmarket staff members ensure the produce is fresh and of high quality – many of the farms are certified organic.

INFORMATION

- ☎ 212-460-1200
- 🖳 www.union-squarenyc.org
- ✉ 223 E 14th St btwn Second & Third Aves
- 🕗 8am-6pm Mon, Wed, Fri & Sat
- € 4, 5, 6, N, R to 14th St
- ♿ good
- ✗ Patria (p73)

The Union Sq Greenmarket is the granddaddy of them all. During peak season (late summer/early fall) there can be as many as 80 farmers and food producers selling organic and nonorganic fruits and vegetables (triple-washed organic lettuces, sugar snap peas, heirloom tomatoes, hot and sweet peppers, fresh corn and carrots), meats and poultry, as well as fresh milk, Pennsylvania Dutch homemade pretzels, hydroponic tomatoes and lettuce, fresh fish from Long Island, vegetable-dyed wool,

Green Light

Electronic cable cars once barreled through Union Sq at nine miles an hour to avoid stalling at a particularly sharp turn on the western edge. So few conductors did it without striking pedestrians that the spot was nicknamed 'Dead Man's Curve,' although it seems women and horses bore the brunt of the punishment.

Hot'n'spicy at Union Sq Greenmarket

beeswax candles, and the list goes on and on. Devoted urbanites gather on market days to browse and purchase the finest selection of farm goods available, including homemade breads and pies, cider and preserves, and numerous other items (depending on the season). If you look closely, you might see a celebrity chef or two among the market's buyers. The market is on Union Sq's west side, just a few steps north of the statue of Ghandi 'striding toward peace.'

HUDSON RIVER PARK (3, B5)

An ambitious project that grew out of unheralded cooperation between environmentalists, developers and politicians, the Hudson River Park Act of 1998 put aside extensive portions of Manhattan's western waterfront exclusively for public recreation. Five miles of smooth walkways stretching from Lower Manhattan to above 59th St offer perfect conditions for bike riding, in-line skating and all sorts of sporty activities. Stretching up to 1,000ft into the Hudson River, 13 rebuilt piers allow park visitors to leave the city behind them and experience the light, water and open space that are unique to the riverfront. And it gives **New York Water Taxis** (p114), the latest innovation in urban island travel, a great place to moor while picking up fares – no gridlock in sight!

INFORMATION
- ☎ 212-533-7275
- 💻 www.hudsonriver park.org
- ✉ Pier 40 at Houston & West Sts
- $ free
- 🚇 trains that run up the West Side, 1, 9, 2, 3 or A, C, E will get you closest
- ♿ excellent
- 🍴 kiosks

Exercise 'til you drop on Hudson River Path

DON'T MISS
- The helicopter collection in the Intrepid museum features two UH-1 Hueys.
- Chelsea Brewing Company at Pier 59 has 24 microbrewed beers.
- Bateaux New York is the most elegant of the Spirit Cruises out of Chelsea Piers.
- Riverflicks shows PG-13 films outdoors at Pier 24 on Wednesdays and Pier 25 on Fridays at dusk.

Get off at Pier 84 and walk up to Pier 86 to check out the **Intrepid Sea-Air-Space Museum** (2, A8), the world's largest naval exhibit comprised of an immense aircraft carrier (the **Intrepid**), a submarine (the **Growler**) and a retired **Concorde** jet. It's a look at the military service experience above and below water, in times of peace as well as war.

The star in all this is **Chelsea Piers** (3, A3), a 30-acre sports and recreation complex (as well as a working TV and film production studio) between 23rd and 17th Sts. Ice-skating, batting cages, playing fields, baseball, basketball, bowling, golf, kayaking, rock climbing and so many more activities are available, as well as a marina offering harbor cruises and sailing instruction. The latest additions include a day spa and child care center.

EMPIRE STATE BUILDING (3, C1)

What a sight! From the 86th floor of the Empire State Building, New York City stretches forth in all its glorious immensity – and it only takes a 45-second elevator ride to reach the heights. With the World Trade Center towers gone, this Art Deco classic has once again become the tallest building in New York and its vivid spire, bathed in a different color combination every night, is a graceful and much loved icon of the city skyline.

INFORMATION

☎ 212-736-3100

▣ www.esbnyc.com

✉ 350 Fifth Ave at 34th St

$ $12/7, children under 5 free; CityPass

⏱ 9am-midnight (last elevator goes up at 11:15pm)

⊕ 6 to 33rd St-Park Ave Sth

♿ good

✕ Empire State Deli; eateries at concourse level

Conceived during the prosperous 1920s, the building didn't actually get built until after the stock market crash of 1929. Thrown up in just 410 days for $41 million, the 102-story landmark opened in 1931 and immediately became the most exclusive business address in the city. Of course, very few could afford the equally exclusive rent: the building sat empty for many years, earning it the early nickname

DON'T MISS

- Six gallery windows in the spacious lobby exhibit art from other city attractions and museums.
- The 34th St lobby showcases eight 3D panels on the seven wonders of the ancient world and the Empire State Building.
- Stunning Art Deco elevators whiz you upstairs so fast your head spins, but take a moment to enjoy their opulence.

Aspire to new heights

'Empty State Building.' The building was also meant to serve as a zeppelin mooring mast but the Hindenburg disaster put a stop to that plan. Luckily for the owners the building was an immediate success with the public, who came in droves to gape at the magnificent city views from the 86th and 102nd floor observatories. A staggering 35,000 people still visit daily, although the 102nd floor observatory has been closed to the public since 1999. To beat the crowds come very early or late, or buy a combination ticket to the **New York Skyride**; that line is usually shorter.

TIMES SQUARE (2, C8)

This maelstrom of human activity and flashing neon lights is definitely the city's most famous intersection. Synonymous in the 1960s with sex shops, peep shows and colorful offbeat characters, today's Times Sq has a comparatively squeaky clean image, thanks mostly to the citywide cleanup of the 1990s. But the trademark high-energy theater buzz still abounds, especially on a weekend night when the lights are flashing, sidewalks are popping, and everybody's hustling to make that 8pm curtain.

Formerly a horse-trading center known as Long Acre Sq, the area was changed forever in 1904 by the advent of the subway. The *New York Times* newspaper moved in (changing the name to Times Sq) and on December 31 held a massive celebration that has become the annual New Year's Eve ball-dropping bacchanalia. No need to link your visit to any particular day though – the full-on high wattage effect of Times Sq is everpresent, with every square inch covered with lights hawking something (zoning laws actually require

INFORMATION

- ☎ 212-768-1560
- 💻 www.timessquare bid.org
- ✉ junction 42nd St, Seventh Ave & Broadway
- ℹ Times Sq Alliance, 1560 Broadway, btwn 46th & 47th Sts, 8am-8pm (information, theater tickets, free Internet access, exchange facilities); free 2hr walking tour (Fri noon)
- 🚇 any train 42nd St-Times Sq
- 🚌 M42, M104
- ♿ reasonable
- ✖ everywhere you turn

Times Sq: where neon goes to die

DON'T MISS

- Times Sq Alliance walking tour
- the neon sea at night
- Town Hall (p90) performance space
- gaudy, bawdy 42nd St and the updated New Amsterdam Theater (p87)

buildings to hang ads on exposed space). Now that **MTV** (Music TV Network) has created a huge studio in the square's center with a glass wall overlooking the crowds, tons of young teens spend hours waiting to catch a glimpse of their favorite stars and the square has definitely taken on a youthful tone (aided in part by the ubiquitous Disney Corporation). Called 'the Crossroads of the World' by some, it remains the brashest, boldest piece of in-your-face 'infotainment' the world's ever seen, and there's simply no other public square like it on the planet.

ROCKEFELLER CENTER (2, C8)

The largest privately owned complex in the world and a classified National Landmark, this center was conceived during the Great Depression of the 1930s by oil magnate John D Rockefeller. These 22 acres of prime city real estate – between Fifth and Seventh Aves and West 47th and 52nd Sts – contain numerous gardens, restaurants, barbershops, music stores, banks, doctors' offices, shoe cobblers, pharmacies, bookstores, clothing stores, a post office and one of America's most outstanding public art collections. An estimated quarter of a million people use it daily and whole parts of the complex are connected by underground passageways. It's fast becoming the hub of Midtown, aglow with light and activity day and night. Over 100 works of art sit within the complex, including a major mural in each building – but

INFORMATION

☎ 212-332-6868

🖳 www.rockefellercenter .com, www.radiocity .com, www.nbc.com

✉ 48th to 51st Sts, btwn Fifth & Sixth Aves

$ outdoor area and GE Bldg lobby free

ⓘ Radio City Music Hall tours (☎ 212-632-4041; $15/9; 🕑 10am-5pm Mon-Sat, 11am-5pm Sun); NBC studio tours (☎ 212-664-3700; $17.50/15; 🕑 8:30am-5:30pm Mon-Sat, 9:30am-4:30pm Sun); Rockefeller Center Tour (☎ 212-664-7174; $10/8; 🕑 9:30am-4:30pm)

🚇 F, V, B, D to 47th St-Rockefeller Center

🚌 M27, M50

♿ good

🍴 Rock Center Café, next to the Sunken Garden; Rainbow Grill (p78)

DON'T MISS

- *Atlas* statue sculpted by Lee Lawrie at the entrance of the International Building
- Radio City Music Hall, an Art Deco masterpiece with a grand Wurlitzer organ
- *Prometheus* statue by Paul Manship at the Sunken Garden
- GE Building, where no office is more than 27ft (8m) from a window

not the mural painted by Mexican artist Diego Rivera for the lobby. Rivera included Lenin in the mural, which did not please his capitalist sponsor. The mural was covered for the opening ceremonies and then later destroyed, to be replaced by Jose Maria Sert's **painting of Abraham Lincoln**.

Rockefeller has a number of prestigious tenants and is something of a communications capital. The TV network **NBC** is headquartered there, as are several leading publishing companies (McGraw-Hill, Simon & Schuster, Time Warner). In winter the main plaza is turned into an ice-skating rink.

FIFTH AVENUE (2, D7–9)

NYC shopping in all its glory parades along Fifth Ave, where strings of tempting, tantalizing stores will turn your head left and right. Once the home of prominent families who lived in gracious, stately mansions, it was taken over by the retail industry in the early 1900s and is now forever associated with fine shopping. Luxury stores abound but increasingly room

INFORMATION

- ☎ 212-484-1222
- ✉ from the Empire State Building on 34th St to Grand Army Plaza on 59th St; 1 mile (1.6km)
- Ⓔ 6 to 33rd St-Park Ave Sth

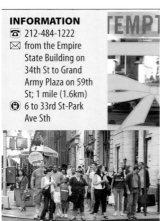

Now where am I again? Oh yeah, Fifth Ave.

is being made for all types – some discount chains have moved in and sit cheek-to-jowl with classics like **Brooks Brothers**, **Bergdorf Goodmans** and **Cartier**. Nowadays the most over-the-top fixture on Fifth Ave is **Trump Tower**, a gleaming complex of exclusive condominiums accessed through a lobby replete with cascading waterfalls, moving stairways, busy cafés and high-end boutiques.

DON'T MISS

- Tiffany & Company's window displays, the epitome of understated elegance
- Saks Fifth Avenue's decorating changes in the 1924 building, the harbingers of changing seasons
- Lord and Taylor, which wins hearts every Christmas for its works-of-art windows
- a stroll down the heart of Fifth Ave from 59th St to 34th St

Just up the street **Grand Army Plaza** gives a glimpse of how the well-heeled lived at the turn of the 19th century. Presided over by the **Plaza Hotel** (2, D7), this romantic square abuts Central Park and is filled with hansom cab drivers ready to take you on a laid-back spin around town. The beaux-arts facades and gray stone fixtures are from a long-ago era, but still undeniably lovely. Other architectural examples of days gone by can be seen at **St Patrick's Cathedral** (2, D7) and the **New York Public**

Watches and jewels and diamonds, oh my!

Library (2, D9). Many designer label stores have reclaimed parts of 57th St on either side of Fifth Ave – **Luis Vuitton** has moved in, as has **Yves Saint Laurent**, **Christian Dior**, **Burberry** and **Chanel**. Around these glossy names sit several swanky art galleries and plush day spas offering relief for the footsore.

MUSEUM OF MODERN ART (2, C7)

A massive renovation led by Japanese architect Yoshio Taniguchi (completed in late 2004) has radically changed the Museum of Modern Art (MoMA) both inside and out. The stylish former entrance, marked by a piano-shaped canopy, now connects to the museum restaurant, while a new main entrance has opened up on West 54th St, between two additions that have nearly doubled the overall square footage. The MoMA now has an eight-story **Education and Research Center** and a **Gallery Building**, which houses all the main galleries including one floor devoted entirely to contemporary art.

All this innovation has only made the brilliance of MoMA's permanent collection more apparent. From an initial gift of eight prints and one drawing in 1929, MoMA now has 135,000 paintings, sculptures, drawings, prints, photographs and design models. MoMA also places special emphasis on film, with regular

INFORMATION
- ☎ 212-708-9400
- 🖳 www.moma.org
- ✉ 11 W 53rd St
- 💲 US$20/12-16, children under 16 free; suggested donations on Friday after 4pm
- 🕙 10:30am-5:30pm Sat-Mon, Wed & Thu, 10:30am-8pm Fri, closed Tue
- ⓘ free guided tours, audio tours $6; tours for visually handicapped and assistive listening devices available
- Ⓔ E, 6 to 51st St-Lexington Ave;
- Ⓟ parking available
- ♿ wheelchairs available; fully accessible
- 🍽 cafeteria, café, bar

PS1
Housed in an abandoned high school, this MoMA affiliate situated in Queens (☎ 718-784-2084; www.ps1.org; 22-25 Jackson Ave, Long Island City) is dedicated solely to contemporary art. PS1 likes flamboyant interactive works (one notable year it featured nude sauna installations open to the public), and Warm Up, its weekly summer music festival, draws thousands.

screenings (free with your museum admission) from its archive of 22,000 titles, plus an immense collection of movie posters. Still, it's the depth of early modern art that really astounds. Not only can you see van Gogh's *Starry Night* here, and Picasso's *Les Demoiselles d'Avignon,* but all three of Umberto Boccioni's *States of Mind,* two Constantin Brancusi works, a Giorgio de Chirico, several offerings from Max Ernst, plenty of Giacomettis, Warhols, Matisses, and the list just goes on and on and on. The MoMA frequently rotates exhibits and pictures with other museums, so if there's one work you particularly want to see, contact the Visitor Services Department in the lobby or by phone (☎ 212-708-9500).

METROPOLITAN MUSEUM OF ART (2, D4)

A lifetime might be just long enough to properly appreciate the nearly three million permanent works of the 'Met.' With a collection ranging from the Paleolithic era to modern times, this truly is one of the world's greatest cultural institutions. The European painting galleries above the marble staircase at the Fifth Avenue entrance could easily consume a day, as could the **Egyptian gallery** (with its perfectly preserved mummies and entire **Temple of Dendur**, saved from submersion in the waters of the Aswan Dam) and the **Greek and Roman** galleries. Behind the Temple is the **American** wing with its incongruous combination of Tiffany glass,

INFORMATION

- ☎ 212-535-7710
- 💻 www.metmuseum.org
- ✉ Fifth Ave at 82nd St
- 💲 suggested donation US$12/7, children under 12 free
- 🕙 9:30am-5:30pm Tue-Thu & Sun, 9:30am-9pm Fri & Sat, closed Mon
- ℹ️ free guided tours, audio tours $6; tours for visually handicapped and assistive listening devices available
- 🚇 4, 5, 6 to 86th St
- 🚌 M1-5
- 🅿 parking available
- ♿ wheelchairs available; fully accessible, must enter through 81st St entrance
- ✖ cafeteria, café, bar

The Cloisters

Set on four acres overlooking the Hudson River, this marvelous extension of the Met (4, A1; ☎ 212-923-3700; www.metmuseum.org) was built in medieval architectural style and provides a lovely setting for an immense collection of Romanesque sculptures, illuminated manuscripts and paintings. Don't miss the **Hunt of the Unicorn** tapestries, the **Merode Triptych** or the serene and well-tended gardens.

baseball cards and the entire facade of a US bank. The dark and lovely **Medieval** galleries appear next, filled with iconic artifacts, Byzantine enamels and religious jewelry. Off to one side is the calm oasis of the **Lehman Wing**, filled with Renaissance paintings by Rembrandt, Memling and El Greco. There's also the **Africa, Oceania and the Americas** galleries, **Asian** art gallery and many special collections. Visiting the Met can be a gorgeous and life-affirming experience but don't try to do too much in one trip. If timing permits, do like New Yorkers and visit on a weekend evening. The museum tends to be less crowded, plus there's the advantage of rooftop bar service and live music.

CENTRAL PARK (2, C1–6)

Hundreds of green spots populate New York City but none holds a candle to Central Park, one of the world's greatest landscaped spaces.

Right in the heart of Manhattan this oasis of rolling pastures and gardens stretches from Midtown up to the beautifully restored **Harlem Meer** (that's Dutch for 'lake'). Walkers, in-line skaters, bikers and joggers share the ample supply of roadways. Couples and friends meet at **Bethesda Fountain** on **Bethesda Terrace**. **Delacorte Theater** presents 'Shakespeare in the Park' every July and August and **SummerStage** has a wildly popular series of outdoor music and dance events.

So much communing with nature gets done in Central Park that it's hard to believe it's almost entirely artificial – in fact it was the first landscaped park in the US. Frederick Law Olmstead and

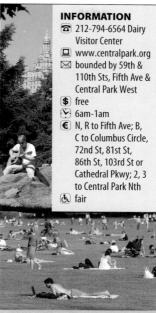

INFORMATION
- ☎ 212-794-6564 Dairy Visitor Center
- 🖳 www.centralpark.org
- ✉ bounded by 59th & 110th Sts, Fifth Ave & Central Park West
- 💲 free
- 🕑 6am-1am
- Ⓔ N, R to Fifth Ave; B, C to Columbus Circle, 72nd St, 81st St, 86th St, 103rd St or Cathedral Pkwy; 2, 3 to Central Park Nth
- ♿ fair

DON'T MISS
- Yoko Ono's Strawberry Fields memorial garden for John Lennon
- the Conservatory Garden's formal fountains and flowering trees
- free summer concerts on the Great Lawn
- the Wildlife Conservation Center and its three climate zones
- beautiful hikes and prime bird-watching in The Ramble on the north side

Laptop Central

Calvert Vaux drew up their vision in 1857 and work got started right away on razing surrounding homes and businesses. A swamp was drained and five million cubic yards of soil moved. Four transverse roads were designed to carry crosstown traffic beneath the park's hills; so natural are the settings that many park goers don't even know that 66th, 79th, 86th and 96th Sts are running underneath them. Wild overgrowth has deliberately been allowed to dominate the northern portion of the park, while the southern section is much more regimented. **Belvedere Castle** (near 79th St) sits valiantly atop Vista Rock, offering great views in all directions, especially over the **Great Lawn**. Some New Yorkers call Central Park the heart of Manhattan and others call it the lungs, but everyone agrees it's a vital part of New York City life.

UNITED NATIONS (2, E8)

This 'international zone' is not officially a part of the United States or New York City – which may be why the city-wide smoking ban is so flagrantly flouted in building cafés! Sitting on 18 riverside acres, the UN buildings and the surrounding park and plaza are quietly impressive. Sculptures donated by member nations and a beautiful rose garden flank the delightful promenade that runs alongside the water.

INFORMATION

- ☎ 212-963-8687
- 🖥 www.un.org
- ✉ 46th St and First Ave
- 💲 free
- ℹ free tours every 20 minutes from 9:30am-4:45pm; for tours in a language other than English call ☎ 212-963-8687 the day before visiting
- Ⓔ any train to 42nd St-Grand Central
- 🚌 M15
- ♿ good
- 🍴 numerous cafés inside

Completed in 1953 by an international team of architects (including Le Corbusier, whose influence is very visible) the tall, green glass **Secretariat Building** forms the center of the complex, backed by the domed **General Assembly Building** and the **Dag Hammarskjöld Library**. When the General Assembly is in session from mid-September to mid-December the flags of all the member nations fly in alphabetical order out front. Security has been tightened in recent years but the UN remains open to the public and still offers

Bureaucracy in a box: the UN building

DON'T MISS

- Delegates Dining Room does a bang up lunch on weekdays (jackets required for men; reservations one day in advance, ☎ 212-963-7625) for about $20.
- Dag Hammarskjöld Plaza across First Ave has great views of the complex.
- The UN post office, which mails your cards with a UN stamp.

its fascinating hour-long guided tour (given in 20 languages) every 30 minutes from the General Assembly lobby. Displays on nuclear energy, war, the environment and other topics are everywhere – corridors are filled with incredible artwork from around the world. A peek into open-door meetings shows how very dated the technology and decor is; the sight of buttoned-down diplomats listening intently through tinny little earphones made c 1970 never fails to raise a chuckle. The UN has a lot of charm considering its bureaucratic roots, thanks to its unique international flavor.

HARLEM (1)

A mecca of urban African-American life for more than 100 years, Harlem has only just begun to reclaim the cultural and artistic status it enjoyed before the Great Depression of the 1930s. Modern Harlem was born when Irish, Italian and Jewish families moved uptown in droves in the 1890s, investing their savings in ornate and gorgeous townhouses. But when the northward movement stopped, developers were left with empty houses to fill. Black families from the rural south were happy to bridge the gap, and by the 1920s Harlem was the most famous black community in the country.

Award-winning poet Langston Hughes, acclaimed novelist Zora Neale Hurston and musicians like Louis Armstrong and Duke Ellington were just some of the names

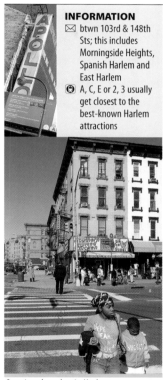

INFORMATION

✉ btwn 103rd & 148th Sts; this includes Morningside Heights, Spanish Harlem and East Harlem

🚇 A, C, E or 2, 3 usually get closest to the best-known Harlem attractions

DON'T MISS

- The Abyssinian Baptist Church, one of the oldest and most influential in the country, has a fabulous gospel choir on Sunday.
- Malcolm Shabazz Mosque/Harlem Market features a vibrant African market and Senegalese restaurants.
- Aaron Davis Hall (1, B1) offers jazz and sponsors a film series.

to emerge from the Harlem Renaissance, an amazing flowering of artistic talent that grew out of the Roaring Twenties. The stock mar-

Crossing the zebra in Harlem

ket crash of 1929 sent Harlem spiraling downward until, largely overlooked by city politicians, it erupted in explosive rage during the 1960s Civil Rights movement. Tense years followed, but now Harlem is undergoing its second Renaissance, restoring its city streets one block at a time. The **Apollo Theater** (1, C2), **Lenox Lounge** (1, C2) and **Cotton Club** (1, A2) are once again pulling people uptown for raucous jazz nights; the **Studio Museum** (1, C2) and **Schomburg Center of Black Research** (1, C1) are two of many cultural magnets. Former US president Bill Clinton's office is on W 125th St and since he moved in, brownstone and apartment rental rates have skyrocketed, one sure sign that a neighborhood is up and coming.

BRONX ZOO/WILDLIFE CONSERVATION PARK (4, B1)

Giving new meaning to the term 'urban jungle,' this 265-acre spread works hard to entertain and educate visitors while preserving the natural needs and rhythms of the animals it houses. More than 4,500 creatures, totaling more than 600 species, roam through mostly unfenced outdoor settings, often separated from the public by nothing more than a moat or other natural barrier. Opened in 1899, the Bronx Zoo has survived by changing with the times – technology and sustainability play big roles in the park's success, as can be seen in one of the latest additions, the **Congo Gorilla Forest**. This six-and-a-half acre re-creation of an African rain forest has treetop lookouts, natural pathways, over-flowing greenery and about 300 animals, including two troops of lowland gorillas and some red river hogs.

INFORMATION
- ☎ 718-367-1010
- 💻 http://wcs.org; www.bronxzoo.com
- ✉ Fordham Rd at Bronx River Pkwy, the Bronx
- 💲 $11/8, free Wed; Congo Forest & rides extra
- 🕐 10am-5pm Mon-Fri, 10am-5:30pm Sat, Sun & holidays, to 4:30pm Nov-Mar
- Ⓔ 2 to Pelham Pkwy, 5 to E 180th St
- 🚃 MetroNorth Getaway packages (☎ 532-4900)
- 🚌 Liberty Lines (☎ 718-652-8400) BxM11 Express from Madison Ave
- 🚗 Exit 6 from Bronx River Pkwy
- ♿ excellent
- 🍴 cafés and snack stands available on-site

DON'T MISS
- Wild Asia: 40 acres for tigers and elephants
- Tiger World: nirvana for big cats in a re-created Amur Valley
- World of Darkness: what goes bump in the night? You'll find out here.
- Butterfly Zone: more than 1,000 fluttery friends
- Jungle World: primal settings for tapirs, gibbons and tree kangaroos

Admission fees go toward caring for the Zoo's animals and toward Wildlife Conservation Society projects around the world. The Bronx Zoo often takes in wounded, sick or endangered animals that WCS partner programs have discovered in the wild. Three different rides – monorail, aerial tram, and shuttle – offer different perspectives of the park. The WCS also runs the **Queens Zoo**, **Prospect Park Zoo** and **Central Park Zoo**. All of them are equally committed to providing animals safe shelter in naturalistic settings, but for sheer size none can rival the mammoth Bronx set-up, which keeps getting bigger and better every year. Children in particular adore the mini-zoo built to their scale with lots of hands-on features. No biting allowed!

Sights & Activities

MUSEUMS

New York's cultural cup runneth over when it comes to fabulous art. Just about every museum has one day (or a few hours on a given day) when regular admission fees are suspended and 'suggested donations' (meaning you pay what you wish) are the norm.

American Museum of Natural History (2, B4) Wander around this behemoth amid the glories of nature. 'Please Touch' signs dot the main floor, free tours are available, the Barosaurus exhibit looms large and the Hall of Biodiversity stresses environmental protection. Special multimedia displays are in vivid color and detail, kids love the Discovery Room and new exhibits evolve all the time.
☎ 212-769-5100
🖳 www.amnh.org
✉ Central Park West at 79th St $ suggested donation $12/7, special exhibits or IMAX shows $19/11, child under 2 free 🕙 10am-5:45pm Ⓑ B, C to 81st St ⓓ good; wheelchairs available

El Museo del Barrio (2, D2) Recent Met and MoMA partnerships have created scintillating exhibits of modern Latin American and Caribbean art, but the permanent exhibit of carved pre-Colombian wooden saints, Mexican masks and local artwork has been a multicultural crowd pleaser for 30 years.
☎ 212-831-7272
🖳 www.elmuseo.org
✉ 1230 Fifth Ave at 104th St in the Heckscher Bldg $ suggested donation $6/4, entry plus audio guide $8, child under 12 free, senior free on Thu 🕙 11am-5pm Wed-Sun Ⓑ 6 to 103rd St, 2, 3 to 110th/Lenox Ave ⓓ good; accessible through Fifth Ave, wheelchairs at front desk

Frick Collection (2, D5) Gorgeous Titian portraits of flame-haired women and delicate Vermeer masterpieces abound in this outstanding private collection of Old Masters. The 1914 mansion is one of the robber baron homes that once made up 'millionaires' row' on Fifth Avenue.
☎ 212-288-0700
🖳 www.frick.org ✉ 1 E 70th St at Fifth Ave $ $12/5-8, incl artphone guide, children under 10 not admitted, children 11-16 in the company of an adult 🕙 10am-6pm Tue-Sat, 1-6pm Sun Ⓑ 4, 5, 6 to 86th St ⓓ excellent

The Jewish Museum (2, D3) Artifacts, dioramas and videos explore Jewish life and art, past and present. The changing exhibits focus on prominent Jews (eg Modigliani), Jewish communities (eg Morocco) and art. A large theater shows films and TV shows.
☎ 212-423-3200
🖳 www.thejewish museum.org ✉ 1109 Fifth Ave at 92nd St $ $12/7.50, child under 12 free; 5-9pm Thu suggested donation 🕙 11am-

5:45pm Mon-Wed, 11am-9pm Thu, 11am-5pm Fri; some exhibits shown at night for a fee, reservations required Ⓑ 4, 5, 6 to 86th St ⓓ excellent; wheelchairs at front desk

Lower East Side Tenement Museum (3, E6) A variety of detailed and evocative tours through tenement buildings give you a good grasp of immigrant life c 1900. The Confino Family tour is great for kids.
☎ 212-431-0233
🖳 www.tenement.org
✉ 90 Orchard St at Broome St $ $12/10, child under 5 free, discounts available for combo-tour tickets 🕙 Visitor Center 11am-5:30pm; museum tours generally every 40min from 1pm & 1:20pm until 4:30pm & 4:45pm Tue-Fri (reservations suggested) Ⓑ B, D to Grand St, F to Delancey St or J, M, Z to Essex St ⓓ fair; Visitor Center is accessible, tenement museums are not

Museum of the City of New York (2, D2) A complete collection of Currier and Ives lithographs and displays of toys, clothes, paintings and costumes from New York's past make this an enjoyable and informative museum. The American Theater collection is a stand out.
☎ 212-534-1672

🖥 www.mcny.org
✉ 1220 Fifth Ave at 103rd St 💲 suggested donation $7/4, family $12 🕑 10am-5pm Tue-Sun 🚇 6 to 103rd St, 2, 3 to 110th-Lenox Ave ♿ fair; access through 104th St entrance

National Museum of the American Indian (3, C8)
A Smithsonian museum celebrating the heritage and achievements of indigenous culture. Exhibits, films, lectures, informal discussions and touch-screen multimedia programs are all used to tell the story of Native Americans. The museum's resource center allows children to handle authentic objects.
☎ 212-514-3700
🖥 www.nmai.si.edu
✉ 1 Bowling Green at Alexander Hamilton US Customs House 💲 free 🕑 10am-5pm Fri-Wed, 10am-8pm Thu 🚇 4, 5 to Bowling Green, 1, 9 to South Ferry, M, J, Z to Broad St ♿ excellent

Skyscraper Museum (3, C8)
An innovative museum dedicated to urban construction; exhibits here are displayed on tall, circular glass columns surrounded by mirrors to create the illusion of vertiginous height. Both the building and the displays are marvelous odes to Manhattan's vertical artistry.
☎ 212-968-1961
🖥 www.skyscraper.org
✉ 39 Battery Park City 💲 $5/2.50 🕑 noon-6pm Wed-Sun 🚇 4, 5 Bowling Green, 1, 9 to Rector St or South Ferry, R, W to Whitehall St ♿ good

Solomon R Guggenheim Museum (2, D3)
Come for the Frank Lloyd Wright spiral interior, come for the fabulous Kandinsky paintings, but come you must. Major works by Brancusi, Klee, Chagall and others form the core of the permanent exhibit. The Thannhauser collection has lovely works from French modernists and the Mapplethorpe photography display, which hangs in a separate gallery space, radiates intimacy from tightly focused portraits.
☎ 212-423-3500
🖥 www.guggenheim .org ✉ 1071 Fifth Ave at 89th St 💲 $15, children under 12 free; suggested donation after 6pm Fri night 🕑 10am-5:45pm Sat-Wed, 10am-8pm Fri 🚇 4, 5, 6 to 86th St ♿ excellent; wheelchairs available

Studio Museum in Harlem (1, C2)
As much a community center as art center, the Studio Museum is a leading showcase of African-American talent with a well-respected artist-in-residence program. 'Hoofer's House' recreates the tap dance genius of the

1920s and James Van Der Zee's magnificent photos of the Harlem Renaissance are on display.
☎ 212-864-4500
🖥 www.studiomuseum .org ✉ 144 W 125th St at Adam Clayton Powell Blvd 💲 suggested donation $12/7/3, child under 12 free 🕑 noon-6pm Wed-Fri & Sun, 10am-6pm Sat 🚇 2, 3 to 125th St, 4, 5, 6 to 125th-Lexington Ave ♿ fair

Whitney Museum of American Art (2, D5)
Specializing in contemporary American art, the Whitney Museum's biennial exhibition of up-and-comers never fails to stir up controversy; its digital shows keep one foot firmly in the future while the permanent display (featuring Pollocks, Rothkos and Hoppers) is legendary.
☎ 212-570-3676, 1-800-WHITNEY
🖥 www.whitney.org
✉ 945 Madison Ave at 75th St 💲 $12/9.50, child under 12 free, suggested donation 6-9pm Fri 🕑 11am-6pm Wed-Thu, Sat & Sun, 1-9pm Fri 🚇 6 to 77th St ♿ good; wheelchairs available

Brooklyn Museum of Art
New York's second-biggest art **museum** (6, B4; ☎ 718-638-5000; 200 Eastern Pkwy; www.brook lynart.org) has excellent collections (58 works by Rodin) and avant-garde sensibilities that sometimes tweak the city's more conservative forces (former mayor Rudolph Giuliani wanted to slash museum funds over a work involving elephant dung and the Virgin Mary).

GALLERIES

For a quick rundown of what's on where, pick up a *Gallery Guide* (available free at most galleries) or a copy of the *Village Voice* (free at newsstands), which has weekly updates and reviews. *Time Out New York* also has extensive coverage (available for a fee at newsstands) and the Sunday *New York Times* also has a good listing of schedules.

Chelsea

Barbara Gladstone Gallery (3, A2) There's plenty of space and natural light in this gallery, and it's often given over to just one artist, either for an exhibit of multiple works or one big installation, as done for Vito Acconci and his multimedia installation, *Spoken Rooms*.
☎ 212-206-9300
🖥 www.gladstonegal lery.com ✉ 515 W 24th St 💲 free 🕑 11am-6pm Tue-Sat Ⓔ C, E, 1, 9 to 23rd St ♿ fair

Caren Golden (3, A2) Not long on the scene but catching a lot of attention, Caren Golden has an eye for young talent: Seong Chun, Jean Blackburn, Paul Henry Ramirez and many others are proud to hang their artwork here.
☎ 212-727-8304
🖥 www.carengolden fineart.com ✉ Ste 215, 526 W 26th St 💲 free 🕑 11am-6pm Tue-Sat Ⓔ C, E, 1, 9 to 23rd St ♿ fair

Clementine (3, A2) A great gallery for art world neophytes, Clementine's intimate and friendly space has cutting-edge works from relative unknowns, especially painters and photographers.

☎ 212-243-5937
🖥 www.clementine-gallery.com ✉ Ste 211, 526 W 26th St 💲 free 🕑 11am-6pm Tue-Sat, closed Jul-Aug Ⓔ C, E, 1, 9 to 23rd St ♿ fair

Gagosian (3, A2) High profile *artistes* from the four corners of the world are on display at Gagosian, and the gallery's vast loft space in Chelsea more than does the work justice. Expect to see contemporary work from the likes of Damien Hirst, Cy Twombly and Dexter Dalwood. Private viewings can be arranged, and there's a second location uptown.
☎ 212-741-1111
🖥 www.gagosian.com ✉ Chelsea: 555 W 24th St; Uptown: 980 Madison Ave 💲 free 🕑 10am-6pm Mon-Fri Ⓔ Chelsea: C, E, 1, 9 to 23rd St; Uptown: 6 to 77th St-Lexington Ave ♿ good

Lehmann Maupin (3, A2) A gorgeous gallery that's not afraid of the unconventional, Lehmann Maupin has been making waves since the late 90s. Tracey Emin, Jorge Sasse and Jun Nguyen Hatsushiba are just a few of the best-known names represented by this gallery.
☎ 212-255-2923
🖥 www.lehmannmaupin .com ✉ 540 W 26th St 💲 free 🕑 11am-6pm Tue-Sat Ⓔ C, E, 1, 9 to 23rd St ♿ fair

Mary Boone Gallery (3, A2) Once jailed for handing out live ammunition to gallery goers, Boone continues to shake things up by showing Brice Marden, Leonardo Drew, Hilary Harkness and others at her popular galleries in Midtown and Chelsea.
☎ 212-752-2929
🖥 http://maryboonegal lery.com ✉ Chelsea:

Gallery Crawl

Just how hot is the Chelsea art scene? An average of 15 new galleries opens every month. New Yorkers stay on top of it all with gallery crawls – afternoons, whole days, even entire weekends spent weaving between hot spots (with plenty of stops for food and coffee) on the extreme west side, generally between 20th and 26th Sts but even straying into Midtown. If you want the whirlwind tour, **New York Gallery Tours** (☎ 212-946-1548; www.nygallerytours.com; $15) offers a comprehensive two-hour jaunt.

541 W 24th St; Midtown: 745 Fifth Ave at 57th St $ free 🕑 10am-6pm Tue-Sat ⊕ Chelsea: C, E, 1, 9 to 23rd St; Midtown: B, Q to 57th St ♿ fair

Matthew Marks (3, A3)

One of the first galleries to leave Soho and set up in Chelsea in 1994, Marks has opened up two others along Tenth Ave, one in a renovated knife factory on 24th St, and the other on 21st St. The original site specializes in big names like Ellsworth Kelly and Nan Goldin. ☎ 212-243-0200 🖥 www.matthewmarks .com ⊠ 522 W 22nd St at Tenth Ave $ free 🕑 11am-6pm Tue-Sat ⊕ C, E, 1, 9 to 23rd St ♿ fair; mostly accessible

Soho/Lower East Side

Rivington Arms (3, E5)

Started in 2001 by two recent college grads (one of whom is the daughter of abstract painter Brice Marden), Rivington Arms has put the Lower East Side on the gallery map with its stable of fresh-faced new talent. ☎ 646-654-3213

🖥 www.rivingtonarms .com ⊠ 102 Rivington St $ free 🕑 11am-6pm Mon-Fri, noon-6pm Sat & Sun, closed Aug ⊕ F to Second Ave-Houston St

Ronald Feldman (3, C6)

An important gallery that exhibits contemporary painting, sculpture, installations, drawings, prints, and hosts performances, Ronald Feldman is at the top of the art game in Manhattan. Recent exhibits include Joseph Beuys and Eleanor Antin. ☎ 212-226-3232 🖥 www.feldmangallery .com ⊠ 31 Mercer St $ free 🕑 10am-6pm Tue-Sat ⊕ A, C, E, 1, 9 to Canal St ♿ fair

Spencer Brownstone (3, C6)

Established in 1997, Spencer Brownstone shows contemporary art with a focus on conceptually based works from young artists like Anna Galtarossa and Sven Pahlsson. The exhibitions include installations, photography, painting, sculpture and video. ☎ 212-334-3455 🖥 www.spencerbrown

stonegallery.com ⊠ 39 Wooster St btwn Grand & Broome Sts $ free 🕑 11am-6pm Tue-Sat ⊕ A, C, E to Canal St ♿ fair

Midtown/ Uptown

Pace Wildenstein (2, D7)

The giant gallery in Midtown features modern and contemporary painters (Piet Mondrian, for one). Upstairs is Pace Prints – open racks of prints that you are free to pick over. The Chelsea space concentrates on up-and-coming artists, sculptors, and photographers. ☎ 212-421-3292, 212-929-7000 🖥 www.pace wildenstein.com ⊠ Midtown: 32 E 57th; Chelsea: 534 W 25th $ free 🕑 Midtown: 9:30am-6pm Mon-Thu, 9:30am-4pm Fri; Chelsea: 10am-6pm Mon-Thu, 10am-4pm Fri ⊕ Midtown: 4, 5, 6, N, R, W to 59th St/Lexington Ave; Chelsea: 1, 9 to 23rd St ♿ fair

Zwirner & Wirth (2, D6)

Works by modern masters like Martin Kippenberger, Gordon Matta-Clark and Thomas Ruff are this gallery's bread and butter, as well as group shows of surrealism in the 20th century and European contemporary artists. ☎ 212-517-8677 🖥 www.zwirnerand wirth.com ⊠ 32 E 69th St $ free 🕑 10am-6pm Tue-Sat (Mon-Fri in summer, closed Aug) ⊕ 6 to 68th-Hunter College ♿ fair

NOTABLE BUILDINGS & LANDMARKS

Carnegie Hall (2, C7)

Carnegie Hall is the city's first great concert venue, built in 1891. The legendary hall is visually and acoustically brilliant, as well as enormously tall. Visitors to the top balcony must climb 105 steps (all but the top level can be reached by elevator). Major renovations in 1996 added a new museum.

☎ 212-903-9750
🖳 www.carnegiehall
.org ✉ 881 Seventh Ave at 57th St 💲 $9/3/6; admission to various concerts varies 🕙 visitors must take a tour to see the Hall, offered at 11:30am, 2pm & 3pm Mon-Fri; tickets can be purchased at the box office from 11am-3pm on tour days 🚇 A, B, C, D, 1 to Columbus Circle, N, Q, R, W to 57th St-Seventh Ave, E to Seventh Ave 🚌 M5, M6, M7, M30, M57 & M104 ♿ good

Chrysler Building (2, D8)

Shorter than its fellow Art Deco triumph, the Empire State Building, the laid-back Chrysler Building nonetheless looks so much more significant. Illuminated at night by a simple white light, it is indisputably the gem of the city's skyline. Visitors to William van Alen's masterpiece are restricted to the lobby; the stainless-steel spire is off-limits.

✉ 405 Lexington Ave at 42nd St 🚇 any train to 42nd St-Grand Central Station 🕙 lobby 9am-7pm

Federal Hall National Memorial (3, D8)

A beautiful example of classical architecture, this 1842 building has lots of history (George Washington was sworn in as president here in 1789) and informative exhibits, but its most loved features are the steps outside, where hundreds of people gather daily to take a break and catch some rays.

☎ 212-825-6888
🖳 www.nationalparks
.com/federal_hall_na
tional_memorial.htm
✉ 26 Wall St 💲 free
🕙 9am-5pm; free guided tours throughout the day 🚇 J, M, Z to Broad St (Mon-Fri), 2, 3, 4, 5 to Wall St ♿ fair

Flatiron Building (3, C3)

Daring and sophisticated, with just enough embedded grime to be interesting, the Flatiron is 6ft wide at its apex and expands from there into a limestone wedge. Nicknamed 'Burnham's Folly' (after the architect), people were sure it would topple when construction was completed in 1902. Instead it has become one of the city's most enduring sights and a symbol of the neighborhood, known as the Flatiron District.

✉ intersection of Broadway, Fifth Ave & 23rd St 🚇 N, R, 6 to 23rd St

Grand Central Terminal (2, D8)

The world's largest and busiest train station (76 acres; 500,000 commuters and subway riders daily) is also a gorgeous feat of engineering and architecture. Take in the theatrical beaux art facade from E 42nd St, particularly luminous at night, and then head inside to marvel at gold-veined marble arches and the bright blue domed ceiling, decorated with twinkling, fiber-optic constellations.

☎ 212-340-2210
🖳 www.grandcentral
terminal.com ✉ Park Ave at 42nd St 💲 free
🕙 5:30am-1:30am daily 🚇 any train to 42nd St/Grand Central ♿ excellent

New York Public Library (2, D9)

Sumptuous light brackets, elaborately

Carnegie Hall: New York's busiest concert venue

Towers of (Food) Power

Seven high-end restaurants are spread out through the Time Warner Center. Among the offerings: **Rare** (mains $25-28), a sprawling steakhouse from Jean-Georges Vongerichten; American creative at the homey **Per Se** (☎ 212-823-9335; mains $11-28); French-Asian fusion at **Café Gray** (☎ 212-823-6338; meals $50-75), where Gray Kunz reigns over an open kitchen; and **Masa** (☎ 212-823-9800; tasting menu $300), a Japanese lair with a celebrity following that rivals Nobu's.

decorated ceilings, window bays, doorways and great stairways all lead up to the elaborately decorated Main Reading Room, almost two city blocks in length on the top floor. The Fifth Ave entrance to the imposing white marble beaux art building, designed in 1911, is flanked by two limestone lions, now synonymous with the library itself.
☎ 212-930-0800
🖳 www.nypl.org
✉ Fifth Ave at 42nd St 💲 free 🕑 11am-7:30pm Tue-Wed, 10am-6pm Thu-Sat 🚇 any train to Grand Central Station or 42nd St-Times Sq ♿ excellent

New York Stock Exchange (3, C8) Closed to the public since 9-11, the NYSE building has a portentous facade reminiscent of a Roman temple (often draped with an American flag) that is still a favorite New York photo-op. The Great Depression started here, on 'Black Thursday' in 1929.
☎ 212-656-3000
🖳 www.nyse.com
✉ 8 Broad St at Wall St

🕑 9am-6pm Mon-Fri
🚇 J, M, Z to Broad St (Mon-Fri only), 2, 3, 4, 5 to Wall St ♿ fair

Time Warner Center (2, B7) The city's newest, glossiest complex comprises two massive towers fronted by a series of smaller buildings; it creates the illusion of an urban mountain. Inside are more than 40 shops, the city's largest food market, private residences, jazz venues and numerous spas, restaurants and bars.
☎ 212-484-8000
🖳 www.timewarner .com ✉ 1 Time Warner Center, 10 Columbus Circle btwn 58th & 60th Sts 💲 free 🚇 A, B, C, D, 1, 9 to 59th St/Columbus Circle

Woolworth Building (3, C7) The Woolworth Building starts out typically enough, with a large wide base followed by a narrow shaft, but no other skyscraper in town is capped by a great pyramid! The oversized Gothic details at the top can be seen from the sidewalk and

the ceiling mosaic inside is definitely worth a look.
✉ 233 Broadway btwn Park Pl & Barclay St 💲 free 🕑 lobby 24hr 🚇 4, 5, 6 to City Hall-Brooklyn Bridge ♿ excellent

World Financial Center (3, C8) A thoroughly modern complex of office towers, shopping plazas and eateries, the World Financial Center somehow manages to transcend the fact that it's a commercial enterprise meant to make a profit. The immense structure sustained major damage on 9-11 but is now back, and as beautiful as it was before. Thirty specialty shops overlook the outdoor waterfront plaza with spectacular views of the river.
☎ 212-945-2600
🖳 www.worldfinancial center.com ✉ 200 Liberty St at Church St 💲 free 🕑 24hr 🚇 A, C to Broadway-Nassau, E to WTC-Chambers, J, M, Z to Fulton, N, R, 4, 5, 6 to Brooklyn Bridge-City Hall, 1, 2 to Park Place ♿ excellent

The Gothic Woolworth

HOUSES OF WORSHIP

Cathedral of St John the Divine (2, B1) St John's construction began in 1892, first in Romanesque-style, then later Gothic Revival and it's still not done – check out the sculptors at work! Seat of New York's Episcopal Diocese, it's an important hub of cultural, spiritual and intellectual New York life.
☎ 212-316-7540
🖥 www.stjohndivine.org
✉ 1047 Amsterdam Ave at 112th St 💲 suggested donation $2 🕑 7am-6pm Mon-Sat, 7am-7pm Sun 🚇 1, 9 to 110th St 🚌 M4 to Amsterdam Ave/110th St ♿ good

Eldridge Street Synagogue (3, E6) An enduring tribute to the spirit of first wave Jewish immigrants, the synagogue features 70ft-high vaulted ceilings, immense rose-colored stained glass window and hand-stenciled walls.
☎ 212-219-0888
🖥 www.eldridgestreet .org ✉ 12 Eldridge St btwn Division & Canal Sts 💲 free 🕑 11:30am-2:30pm Tue-Thu, 11am-4pm Sun, or by appointment Mon-Fri
🚇 F to E Broadway, S (shuttle) from W 4th St to Grand St 🚌 9, 15, 22 to East Broadway & Market Sts ♿ fair

Islamic Cultural Center (2, D3) The first mosque and religious center created specifically for New York's Muslim community, the center has a large forecourt

St John, patron saint of tilting cathedrals

where worshipers gather for the call for prayers. Its sleek, rounded dome and minaret support a large carving of a thin crescent moon that stands out dramatically on the Upper East Side skyline.
☎ 212-722-5234
🖥 http://admin.muslims online.com/~iccny/
✉ 1711 Third Ave at 96th St 🕑 11am-7pm Sat-Thu; tours 11am Sat-Thu 🚇 6 to 96th St 🚌 M96 to 96th St ♿ fair

Riverside Church (1, A3) A glorious building modeled mainly after French Gothic structures, Riverside Church has the world's largest set of carillon bells. Martin Luther King Jr., Nelson Mandela and Fidel Castro have all graced the podium.
☎ 212-870-6700
🖥 www.theriverside churchny.org ✉ 490 Riverside Drive at 120th St 💲 free 🕑 7am-10pm via Claremont Ave entrance; visitor's center open 10am-7pm Wed 🚇 1, 9 to 116th St 🚌 M104, M4, M5 to 120th or 122nd St ♿ good

St Patrick's Cathedral (2, D7) Across from Rockefeller

Center, with its two soaring 330ft spires, St Patrick's is a spectacular architectural sight. Modeled on a mix of Gothic revival styles, it is the ceremonial heart of the city and the seat of the Roman Catholic Archdiocese of New York.
☎ 212-753-2261 🖥 www .ny-archdiocese.org/past oral/cathedral_about.html
✉ Fifth Ave btwn 50th & 51st Sts 💲 free 🕑 7am-8:45pm 🚇 V to Fifth Ave-53rd St, 4, 6 to 53rd St-Lexington Ave 🚌 M1, M2, M3, M4, M5, Q32 to Fifth Ave/53rd St ♿ fair

Temple Emanu-El (2, D6) A majestic blend of Moorish and Romanesque styles, this temple houses a small but remarkable collection of Judaica. Three galleries tell how Emanu-El grew from a Lower East Side immigrant congregation to a wealthy reform synagogue on Manhattan's Upper East Side.
☎ 212-744-1400
🖥 www.emanuelnyc.org
✉ 1 E 65th St 💲 free 🕑 9am-7pm 🚇 6 to 68th St-Hunter College 🚌 M66 to 68th St-Hunter College ♿ fair

PARKS AND GARDENS

Battery Park (2, C9) Home to 13 works of public art and 35 acres of greenery, this park draws nature- and art-lovers alike. The Jewish Museum's Holocaust Memorial, the NYC Police Memorial and the Irish Hunger Memorial stand out, and Fritz Koenig's *Sphere*, which used to grace the WTC complex, now sits in the rose-filled Hope Garden. ☎ 311 🖥 www.nyc govparks.org ✉ Broadway at Battery Pl $ free ☼ sunrise–1am ❸ 4, 5 to Bowling Green, 1, 9 to South Ferry 🚌 M6, M15 to Staten Island Ferry ♿ good

Bryant Park (3, C1) This flowering haven behind the New York Public Library has chess, backgammon and pétanque (a French game using metal balls) competitions daily, free outdoor film screenings on Monday night, morning concerts on Friday with Latin dancing at night, Broadway shows performed outside, readings from popular authors, and many other cultural events. Thanks

A bit of woof'n'hoof at Tompkins Sq Park

to the in-park restaurant, it's also a popular place to grab an after-work drink. ☎ 212-768-4242 🖥 www.bryantpark.org ✉ Sixth Ave btwn E 40th & 42nd Sts $ free ☼ 7am–11pm Mon-Fri, 7am–8pm Sat & Sun in summer, 7am–7pm Jan-Apr ❸ F, V, B, D to 42nd St-Bryant Park, 7 to Fifth Ave 🚌 M42 to 42nd St-Bryant Park ♿ excellent

Conservatory Garden (2, D2) Near the magnificent Harlem Meer (Dutch for 'lake') on Central Park's northeast corner are six gorgeously landscaped acres: the Central Garden with yew

hedges and crab apple trees, the North Garden with big flower beds in elaborate patterns, and perennials in the luscious South Garden. In spring the Untermeyer Fountain is surrounded by 20,000 blooming tulips. ☎ 212-360-2766 🖥 www.centralparknyc .org ✉ Near Fifth Ave & E 105th St in Central Park $ free ☼ 8am–dusk ❸ 6 to 103rd St 🚌 M96 ♿ fair

Isamu Noguchi Garden Museum (6, A2) More than 240 works, including stone, metal, wood and clay sculptures and models for public projects and gardens are displayed in these tranquil settings, designed by the artist himself. Encircling a garden containing major granite and basalt sculptures, this museum is an art installation in its own right. ☎ 718-204-7088 🖥 www.noguchi.org ✉ 9-01 33rd Rd in Long Island City, Queens $ $5/2.50 ☼ 10am–5pm Wed-Fri, 11am–6pm Sat & Sun ❸ N, W to Broadway in Queens. Walk 10 blocks

Bryant Park Reading Room – bank on it

toward the East River, turn left onto Vernon Blvd. Pass Socrates Sculpture Park & make a left; the museum is two blocks up on the left. ♿ fair

Marcus Garvey Park (1, D3) Noted civil rights activist Marcus Garvey used to preach to the public in this rocky park, one of the oldest in the city, and launched his back-to-Africa movement from the street corners. Along the west side is a row of historical brownstones done in the neoclassical style and an old watchtower (where volunteer firemen used to stand poised to sound the alarm in the event of a fire) still sits in one corner. The park hosts the Charlie Parker Jazz Festival in August, sharing a weekend of music with Tompkins Sq Park. ☎ 311 🖳 www.nyc govparks.org ✉ Fifth Ave btwn W 120th & 124th Sts $ free ⏱ 6am-1am ⊕ 2, 3 to 125th St ♿ fair

Riverside Park (2, A1–5) Nestled between Riverside Dr and the Hudson River, this wooded band of park stretches for 4 miles up Manhattan's west side, affording beautiful views of New Jersey. Playgrounds, sports fields and numerous monuments have been added since it was first built in 1873; Hippo Park Playground at 91st St is one of the best-kept play areas in town and a kid magnet. Adults seem to like it too! ☎ 311 🖳 www.riverside parkfund.org ✉ Riverside Dr from 68th to 155th Sts

Bryant Park: the number one place to watch grass grow

$ free ⏱ 6am-1am ⊕ 1, 2, 3, 9 any stop btwn 66th & 157th Sts ♿ good

Tompkins Square Park (3, E4) This leafy green park has a checkered past. It has witnessed numerous clashes between police and public (the original 1874 Tompkins Sq Riot involved 7000 angry laborers and 1600 police, but there have been many since, usually over gentrification attempts around the park) but was also a preferred haunt of jazz musician Charlie Parker, who lived at 151 Ave B. Every August a Charlie Parker Jazz Festival is held in the park. ☎ 311 🖳 www.nycgov parks.org ✉ E 7th & 10th Sts, bordered by Aves A & B $ free ⏱ 6am-midnight ⊕ 6 to Astor Pl 🚌 M15

to East Village-Houston St ♿ good

Washington Square Park (3, C4) All the world's a stage and everybody's trying out for a bit part in Washington Sq Park, still the bohemian heart of Greenwich Village. Young lovers — gay and straight — congregate to watch the street performances (Bob Dylan sang his first folk song at the fountain, after all) and speed chess is played obsessively into the wee hours. ☎ 212-431-1080 🖳 www.nycgovparks .org ✉ intersection of Fifth Ave & Waverly Pl btwn MacDougal & Wooster Sts $ free ⏱ 6am-1am ⊕ A, C, E, F, V to W 4th St/Washington Sq ♿ good

Northern Exposure
You think you've entered the subway, but it turns out to be a Venetian canal. Is it the humidity? No, it's public art — brought to you by the Public Art Fund, a nonprofit organization that goes to great lengths to pepper city streets with engaging works where you least expect them. Locations of the latest installations are available at ☎ 212-980-4575, www .publicartfund.org.

SQUARES, STREETS & CITYSCAPES

Herald Square (3, C1)
A pretty little square that like most others in Manhattan isn't really a square at all, this genteel triangle has hidden all traces of its sordid past, when it was the heart of a red-light district known as 'The Tenderloin.' The neighborhood gentrified in the early 1900s and now is mainly a shopping district, dominated by the massive Macy's department store. It's the starting point for New York's annual Thanksgiving Day parade featuring huge hot-air balloons and is absolutely jam-packed in the weeks leading up to the Christmas holidays.
☎ 212-922-9393
✉ 34th St, btwn Fifth & Sixth Aves $ free
☼ 24hr ⊖ B, D, F, N, Q, R to 34th St ♿ fair

Little Brazil (2, C8) The smells and sounds of Brazil permeate these streets, but particularly W 46th St, where soccer and samba are staples in every bar.

> ### Hua Mei Bird Garden
> The delicate Chinese art of training Hua Mei birds to sing is on display every morning at Sara Delano Roosevelt Park on the Lower East Side (3, D5), amid plentiful flowers and Tai Chi practitioners. Notice how the fancy bamboo cages are placed in the trees – Hua Mei learn from the sounds of wild birds.

Several of the city's best *churrascaria* restaurants are situated here and the annual Brazilian Day Parade in summer is always a raucous and rowdy event.
✉ W 42nd to 54th Sts btwn Fifth & Seventh Aves ⊖ any train to 42nd St/Times Sq ♿ fair

Little Korea (3, C1–2)
Koreatown, affectionately called 'K-town' by many, is a colorful strip of streets populated by a few lone Japanese supermarkets and tons of Korean delis, restaurants and shops. Some of the best Korean BBQ outside of Queens can be found here.
✉ 31st to 36th Sts btwn Fifth & Sixth Aves ⊖ B,

D, F, N, Q, R at 34th St ♿ fair

Madison Square Park (3, C2) An often overlooked little park opposite the Flatiron Building, this was once an important and bustling area, home to the first Madison Sq Garden building, and the birthplace of president Teddy Roosevelt and writer Edith Wharton. Filled with elegant statues, it's a favorite lunch spot and hosts free summer art programs for kids.
☎ 311 🖥 www.nycgov parks.org ✉ 23rd to 26th Sts btwn Broadway & Madison Ave $ free
☼ 6am-1am ⊖ N, R, 6 to 23rd St ♿ fair

'Yeah, I'm at Herald Square. Near the trash can. OK?'

NEW YORK CITY FOR CHILDREN

The Big Apple is a big hit with kids, and there are tons of attractions and entertainments designed just for them. Parents, however, may find it hard to get on and off subways and buses (subways in particular) laden with strollers, backpacks and offspring. There are gated doors beside the too-skinny-turnstiles at subway exits and entrances; catch the attention of the clerk on duty and they'll buzz you through. New Yorkers generally are quick to lend a hand so don't be surprised if someone helps you navigate the stairs. Some museums don't allow strollers on certain days but will give you baby carriers to make up for it.

Children are mostly welcome everywhere, with a few exceptions: after work (6pm) bars are considered adult-only, which is why New Yorkers started the 'Tots'n'Tonic' trend, a happy hour from 3pm to 5pm, mostly on the Upper East and West Sides, for toddlers and parents. Many restaurants, hotels and attractions are quite happy to cater to families; look for the 🚼 icon listed with general reviews in the Eating, Sleeping and Entertainment chapters for more kid-friendly options.

To make the cultural capital your personal playground, pick up a *Time Out New York Kids,* published four times a year and available at newsstands. It has tons of fabulous information and listings. GoCity Kids is a useful online reference (www.gocitykids.com) as is New York Kids (www.newyorkkids.net).

Bowlmor Lanes (3, C4) Perfect for a rainy day, Bowlmor Lanes has neon pins, lightweight balls for little hands, lots of hip music and, very frequently, celebrity clients. Kids love the whole scene, starting with the elevator ride to get to the 2nd floor lanes.
☎ 212-255-8188
🖳 www.bowlmor.com
✉ 110 University Pl
💲 per person, per game $6.45 (before 5pm weekdays), weekends $8.45, shoes $4 🕙 11am-6pm for kids, 21 & over after 6pm 🚇 any train to Union Sq

Central Park (3, C1–6) Kids shouldn't miss these: **Alice in Wonderland Sculpture** near Fifth Ave and 74th St, **Central Park Wildlife Center** at Fifth Ave and 64th St, **Kerbs Conservatory** at Fifth Ave and 72nd St, where kids sail radio-controlled model yachts, **Central Park Carousel** at 64th St and **Dana Discovery Center** at Fifth Ave and 110th St, which actually has a stocked lake for fishing!
☎ 212-794-6564, visitor center 🖳 www .centralpark.org ✉ from 59th-110th Sts & Fifth Ave to Central Park W
💲 free 🕙 6am-1am

Children's Museum of the Arts (3, D6) No looking allowed! This is a museum of direct participation. Fabulous multi-sensory activities are educational and fun, and conducted under the watchful eyes of facilitators, all trained artists themselves. Warning: children will leave knowing how to make Flubber at home.
☎ 212-274-0986, 212-941-9198 🖳 www .cmany.org ✉ 182 Lafayette St btwn Broome & Grand Sts 💲 $6, suggested donation from 4-6pm Thu 🕙 noon-5pm Fri-Sun & Wed, noon-6pm Thu 🚇 6 to Spring St, N, R to Prince St 🚌 M1 to Broadway & Canal Sts, M6 to Sixth Ave-Houston St 🚹 fair

Mars 2112 (2, C7) Life on Mars in the year 2112 isn't too bad, as you'll find out once you step through

Babysitting

The **Babysitters Guild** (☎ 212-682-0227; www
.babysittersguild.com; 60 East 42nd St; per hr $15,
4hr minimum) has been providing quality child care
in New York for 60 years now, and is still ranked
as the city's best agency. Sixteen languages can be
accommodated. Most hotels also have reliable babysitters on call.

the departure gate in the futuristic lobby of this family-oriented theme restaurant. Adults can sip Martian-brewed beer while kids stare at flying saucers (and the food's good too).
☎ 212-582-2112
🖥 www.mars2112.com
✉ 1633 Broadway at 51st St $ children's meals start at $9
🕑 11:30am-9pm Sun-Thu, 11:30am-10:30pm Fri, 11:30am-9:30pm Sat
🚇 1, 9, A, C to 50th St
🚻 fair

New Victory Theater

(2, C8) The 'family treat on 42nd St' is an elegant, intimate theater sized for wee ones who need to see over Grandma's beehive. This playhouse for kids does all sorts of shows, from Bunraku puppetry to Alvin Ailey performances, and even manages to draw kids in to dramatic plays. Call for seasonal programs.
☎ 646-223-3020
🖥 www.newvictory.org
✉ 209 West 42nd St btwn Seventh & Eighth Aves $ $10-30 🕑 box office 11am-5pm Sun-Mon, noon-7pm Tue-Sat
🚇 any train to 42nd St/Times Sq or Port Authority
🚻 good

The New York Fire Museum (3, C5) and New York City Police Museum

(3, D8) Both these museums are bursting with fascinating paraphernalia. The Fire Museum has hand pumps and a mock apartment blaze that kids can try to put out. The Police Museum's got weird bad-guy stuff (Al Capone's tommy gun) and lots of counterfeit money. Informative but exciting tours offered at both places.
☎ Fire Museum: 212-691-1303; Police Museum: 212-480-3100 🖥 www.nycfiremuseum.org & www.nycpolicemuseum.org ✉ Fire Museum: 278 Spring St btwn Hudson & Varick Sts; Police Museum: 100 Old Slip near South St Seaport $ $6 suggested donation for adults 🕑 Fire Museum: 10am-5pm Tue-Sat, 10am-4pm Sun; Police Museum: 10am-5pm Tue-Sat 🚇 Fire Museum: 1, 9 to Houston, C, E to Spring St; Police Museum: 2, 3 to Wall St 🚻 good

New York Waterway Sightseeing Cruises

(3, A1) Water cruises are the latest craze to hit New York, but only this outfit's created a special 90-minute version just long enough for kids. You won't fully circle Manhattan but you'll hit all the highlights that matter, plus the guides pack in some funny trivia that youngsters enjoy.
☎ 800-533-3779
🖥 www.nywaterway.com ✉ Pier 78 at West 38th St on the Hudson River $ basic tour $20/10/17 🕑 every hr 10am-3pm Mon-Fri, 10am-4pm Sat & Sun in summer; limited service in winter 🚇 A, C, E to 34th St/Penn Station: red, white & blue NY Waterway buses bring you to the pier for free; they run all over town, just wave one down like a cab & jump on 🚻 fair

At Coney Island you too can sit in a giant teacup

QUIRKY NEW YORK

Casa La Femme North (2, E7) Although this is a popular and well-established Egyptian restaurant, anyplace that changes its decor every eight weeks and brings in sand to create a desert look (or sods for the oasis) certainly has an off-beat sensibility. So lean back in your white tent, take a pull on that hookah and send for the dancing girls (they perform nightly).
☎ 212-505-0005
✉ 1076 First Ave at 59th St $ $55 prix fixe, mains $17-$33 ⏲ 5pm-midnight Sun-Tue, 5pm-3am Wed-Sat ⊕ 4, 5, 6, N, R, W to 59th St/Lexington Ave.

Cubby Hole (3, B4) Hang out and have a drink at this friendly bar that's decorated like a children's room. Christmas balls, rubber fish, paper lamps and other card-store decorations hang from the ceiling like an upside-down psychedelic forest. Check out the Bugs Bunny & Co bar stools. No karaoke anymore, but regulars sing along to the jukebox anyway. Lesbian bar with an open/mixed crowd.
☎ 212-243-9041 ✉ 281 West 12th St $ per drink $4-8 ⏲ 4pm-4am Mon-Fri, 2pm-4am Sat & Sun ⊕ 1, 2, 3, 9 to 14th St

Cuddle Party (2, E5) Urban isolation can lead people to do strange things – like attend a cuddle party on the Upper East Side! People who think they may not be getting enough 'touching' in their lives can put on their pajamas and stop in for a group hug – absolutely no sex allowed. Cuddle Lifeguards are on hand to make sure nobody gets in over their head.
☎ 212-737-6368

🖳 www.cuddleparty.com ✉ Apt 5RE 316 E 70th St $ $30 ⏲ check calendar for monthly events ⊕ 6 to 68th St/Hunter College

Fringe Festival This 16-day celebration shows some of the best emerging theater companies and performing artists in the world, and it's held in venues all over the Lower East Side and East Village. Some pretty far-out stuff gets shown, along with the occasional big number like *Urinetown*, which made it onto Broadway in 2004.
☎ 212-279-4488
🖳 www.fringenyc.org ✉ Fringe Central (box office) 127 MacDougal btwn W 3rd & W 4th Sts $ general admission $15, child under 12 going to FringeJR show $8; tickets available online, by phone or at

Coney Island (6, B6)
The birthplace of carnival culture is a hotbed of freaky summer fun:
- **Coney Island Museum** (6, B6; ☎ 718-372-5159; www.coneyisland.com/museum.shtml; 1208 Surf Ave; 99¢; ⏲ 2-5pm Sat-Sun) offers 1940s memorabilia.
- **'Sideshows by the Seashore'** (6, B6; ☎ 718-372-5159; www.coneyisland.com/sideshow.shtml; 1208 Surf Ave; $5; ⏲ 2pm-8pm Wed-Sun) is staffed by some very flexible people.
- The **New York Aquarium** (6, C6; ☎ 718-265-FISH; www.nyaquarium.com; Surf Ave; ⏲ 10:30am-4:30pm) is great for the whole family.
- The Mermaid Day Parade celebrates the June solstice; pagan attire preferred but not required.
- Nathan's July 4th Hot Dog Eating Contest recently set a world record: 53.5 hot dogs eaten in 12 minutes.
- Fireworks are held every Friday at 9:30pm.
- **Astroland Amusement Park** (☎ 718-372-0275; www.astroland.com; 1000 Surf Ave at W 10th St; ⏲ noon-midnight in summer; weekends in spring) is home to the still functioning Cyclone Roller Coaster.
- The Saturday Night Film Festival shows vintage and modern classics for $5.

Yeah – what the sign says

Fringe Central noon-8pm from Aug 6; hrs vary during festival Fringe Central: A, C, E, D, F, V, B to W 4th St fair

Hellfire Club (6, A5) Once upon a time clubs like Hellfire were in Manhattan's Meatpacking District – now you have to head out to Park Slope for a glimpse of the city's darker side. Although the name is a bit scary, Hellfire's a well-respected sex club that welcomes new faces and respects people's boundaries. But it's definitely not your run-of-the-mill drinking establishment!
☎ 718-369-5009
💻 www.hellfireclubny .com ✉ 117 25th St, Park Slope in Brooklyn $ men $35, couples $25, women free 10pm-4am Fri & Sat W, M, R to 25th St & Fourth Ave excellent

The Museum of Sex (3, C2) Some of the more daring exhibits can definitely bring a blush to your cheeks, but overall this is a tasteful look at some of the high jinks humans can get up to when left to their own devices (and speaking of devices – there

is an interesting exhibition of sex toys). Lots of spicy and fresh exhibits keep people coming back.
☎ 212-689-6337
💻 www.museumofsex .com ✉ 233 Fifth Ave at 27th St $ $14.50/13.50 11am-6:30pm Sun-Fri, 11am-8pm Sat (last ticket sold 45min before closing) N, R, 6 to 28th St fair

New York Burlesque Festival New Burlesque is the dernier cri in sophisticated adult entertainment these days, and the annual burlesque festival keeps getting bigger. If you miss this May event, check out the website for ongoing burlesque shows in New York, often at **Avalon** (3, C3; ☎ 212-807-7780; 660 Sixth Ave at 20th St) and the **Pussycat Lounge** (☎ 212-726-1935; www .pussycatlounge.com; 96 Greenwich St). The festival has yet to find a permanent home, but information can be found well in advance on the website.
☎ 917-770-8559
💻 thenewyorkburlesque festival.com ✉ varies $ varies every May

Night of a Thousand Stevies (3, C6) The most notorious Stevie Nicks fan event in the world, this competition is a riot of shawls, twirling, tambourines and great performances. It started in 1991 at the legendary Jackie 60 club (now defunct), and thousands turn out every year to see who does the best Stevie Nicks impersonation. The event almost went

under with Jackie 60 but was rescued by the **Knitting Factory** (www.knitting factory.com), which now lends its space for the annual event.
☎ 212-219-3132
💻 www.mothernyc.com /stevie/ ✉ 74 Leonard St $ varies varies any train to Canal St

Waikiki Wally's (3, E5) A Polynesian outpost on the East Side, Wally's has trotted out every cliché in the book: working waterfall, grass shack, Don Ho–inspired tiny bubbles, birds in huge cages and scantily clad waitresses giving you a 'lei' at the front door. It's quirky all right!
☎ 212-673-8908
💻 www.waikikiwallys .com ✉ 101 E 2nd St at First Ave $ mains $12-30 6-10pm Sun-Thu, 6-11pm Fri & Sat F to Second Ave

Wigstock/HOWL Festival (3, E4) The most famous one-day outdoor drag festival in Manhattan history, Wigstock is a super-sized stage for wigs, lip-synching, real singing, dancing and whips – basically, standard East Village fare. It's now joined forces with the Howl! Festival for the Arts, so expect a few crossover celebrity appearances and look-alikes that will fool you every time.
☎ 212-387-7684, 212-243-3143 💻 www .wigstock.nu & www .howlfestival.com ✉ Tompkins Sq Park $ free late August, exact date varies 6 to Astor Pl, F to Second Ave good

NYC FOR FREE

Savvy visitors know that you don't have to spend a fortune to enjoy New York. The city is bursting with hundreds of no-cost and low-cost pleasures that include concerts, plays, museum exhibitions and tours. The big money-saver is to take advantage of museums' 'suggested donation' hours.

Big Apple Greeter Get a feel for the city through a New Yorker's eyes. These experienced, multilingual local volunteers share the secrets of their favorite neighborhoods for free. Reserve at least three to four weeks in advance to guarantee yourself a spot on a tour.
☎ 212-669-8159
🖳 www.bigapple greeter.org $ free

Dana Discovery Center (2, C1) Located in the northeast corner of Central Park, the center will lend you a pole for an afternoon of catch-and-release fishing in the Harlem Meer, a beautiful lake also frequented by numerous species of wild birds. Take advantage of the center's educational workshops for children, or grab a pair of binoculars and sharpen your bird-watching eye. It's free to all.
☎ 212-860-1370
🖳 www.central parknyc.org ✉ 110th St & Lennox Ave $ free ⏱ 10am-4pm Tue-Sun Apr-Oct Ⓜ 6 to 110th St-Lexington Ave

Museum Mile Festival (2, D2–4) For one day in June every year – rain or shine – all the museums on Fifth Ave from 82nd to 105th Sts are free and the streets are pedestrian-only. Thousands of people 'walk the mile' and enjoy the street art, music and incredible cultural richness of Manhattan.
☎ 212-606-2296
🖳 www.museum milefestival.org ✉ Fifth Ave btwn 82nd & 104th Sts $ free ⏱ 6-9pm Ⓜ 4, 5, 6 to 86th St or 6 to 103rd St

Staten Island Ferry (3, D9) One of the best deals in town, these large, multi-decked ferries offer free, 30-minute rides between Manhattan and Staten Island 24 hours a day. Spacious and comfortable (with beautiful open-air decks in summer), the ferries feature fabulous views of all the big sights – Lower Manhattan, the Brooklyn Bridge and the Statue of Liberty. Once you've docked on Staten Island, you can take a gentle stroll through the quaint community of St George or simply catch the next outbound ferry back to the city.
☎ 718-815-BOAT
🖳 www.nyc.gov/html /dot/html/masstran /ferries/statfery.html ✉ Whitehall Terminal at Whitehall & South Sts $ free ⏱ 24hr Ⓜ 1, 9 to South Ferry

The Art of the Deal

New York offers free warm-weather performances in the city's parks by the **New York Philharmonic** (2, B6; ☎ 212-875-5000; http://newyorkphilharmonic .org), **Metropolitan Opera** (2, B6; ☎ 212-879-5500; www.metopera.org), the **Public Theater's Shakespeare in the Park** (2, C4; ☎ 212-539-8500; www .publictheater.org; Delacorte Theater) and ongoing concerts and film series in **Bryant Park** (2, C9; ☎ 888-NYPARKS, or Central Park Conservancy, www.cen tralparknyc.org). Jazz, tapas and drinks are offered in the **Hayden Sphere** in the **American Museum of Natural History** (p29) on the first Friday of every month, which is a 'pay-what-you-wish' period for the museum. And The **World Financial Center** (p34) in Lower Manhattan frequently offers free outdoor dance and music performances.

Out & About

WALKING TOURS
Literary Greenwich Village

Start in shady **Washington Sq Park** (**1**), making sure to note the famous **arch** (**2**) designed by Stanford White, the big **'Hanging Elm'** (**3**; public execution site pre-1900s) on the northeast corner, and the surrounding brownstones. **No 19** (**4**) belonged to Henry James's family and Edith Wharton lived at **No 7 Washington Sq North** (**5**). Head southwest on former Beat Generation hangout MacDougal St; Louisa May Alcott penned *Little Women* at **No 130** (**6**). When you reach Bleecker St, turn northwest and follow it across Sixth Ave. As Bleecker St crosses Seventh Ave take a left onto Barrow St and follow it to Bedford St. Poet Edna St Vincent Millay and actor John Barrymore lived at **751/2 Bedford**

Food and books: New York essentials

(**7**), the city's narrowest building, and **Chumley's** (**8**), at No 86, hosted F Scott Fitzgerald on many occasions. Head down Barrow St to Hudson St and on to No 567 the **White Horse Tavern** (**9**), where Dylan Thomas drank himself into a mortal stupor. Follow Hudson St north, passing Bank, Bethune, W 12th, and Horatio Sts, noting beautiful **Abingdon Sq** (**10**) on the corner of Bethune and Eighth Ave. At Gansevoort St in the Meatpacking District stop for a bite at **Florent** (**11**) or a relaxing glass of wine at nearby **Rhone**. If you continue on Ninth Ave heading north you will find yourself in the heart of Chelsea.

distance 2.8 miles (4km)
duration 2-3hr
▶ **start** Ⓜ 8th St NYU
⏺ **end** Ⓜ Eighth Ave 14th St

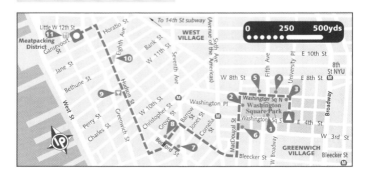

Chinatown into Union Square

Start at Sixth Ave and Canal St and head east along Canal St, detouring into Wooster, Greene and Mercer Sts for Soho galleries **Spencer Brownstone** (**1**), **Deitch Project** (**2**) and **Ronald Feldman** (**3**). Continue on Canal, keeping the Manhattan Bridge on your right. Head northeast on to Allen St, then east on Broome St for one block to see the **Tenement Museum** (**4**), at 90 Orchard St. Then continue north on Allen until, turning east on Rivington St, you reach **Rivington Arms** (**5**) at No 102 and Sara D Roosevelt Park. Walk around its southern edge to Bowery St. Cross Bowery and head into the Nolita quadrant of Lafayette, Spring and Houston Sts. After absorbing the scene, have a drink at **Porcupine** (**6**), then get back on Bowery and go north. Cross Houston and take a right on to E 2nd St, passing **CB-GB's** (**7**), No 315, for a peek at the **New York Marble Cemetery** (**8**). Turn north on to Ave A in historic East Village until you reach **Tompkins Sq Park** (**9**). Grab a bite at **Dawgs on Park** (**10**), then head northwest on E 7th St to No 30, **St George's Ukrainian Church** (**11**). At Third Ave go north one block to **St Mark's Pl** (**12**). Explore this street, and then continue north on Fourth Ave from **Cooper Union** (**13**) to **Union Sq** (**14**).

Psst. You wanna buy a hat?

distance 3.5 miles (5km)
duration 3-4hr
▶ **start** Ⓜ Canal St
⏺ **end** Ⓜ 14th St-Union Sq

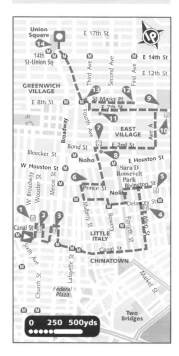

Walking tour weapons of choice

Central Park West to East Side and Museum Mile

Jump on the footpath into Central Park where W 81st St meets Central Park West. Follow the path to the right and head up the incline until you see **Delacorte Theater** (**1**) on your right. The **Great Lawn** (**2**) is visible to your left. Stroll a bit, then retrace your steps towards the drive, turning left at the stairs leading to **Belvedere Castle** (**3**) by way of **Shakespeare Garden** (**4**). From the back of the castle follow the path that runs alongside **Turtle Pond** (**5**), to a stone terrace. Keep the King of Poland statue on your left, walk uphill and head southwest along East Drive to the **Loeb Boathouse** (**6**). Cross the drive and head for the **Alice in Wonderland Statue** (**7**) at the north end of the **Conservatory Pond** (**8**), a good place to have a snack. Exit at 72nd St and Fifth Ave and head for 74th St and Madison Ave to see the **Whitney Museum** (**9**), and then continue up Fifth Ave to the **Met** (**10**) just below 84th St. The **Guggenheim** (**11**) is at 89th St, and you can reenter the park at the 90th St Bridle Path if you wish. To the north is the newly restored **Harlem Meer** (**12**), or exit at 102nd St and Fifth Ave and walk three blocks north to the tranquil **Conservatory Gardens** (**13**).

distance 5.5 miles (9km)
duration 4hr
▶ **start** Ⓜ 81st St-Museum of Natural History
⏺ **end** Ⓜ Cathedral Parkway (110th St)

Central Park triathlon: walk, bike, boat

DAY TRIPS
City Island (5, B2)

It's quite a shock to cross the tiny blue bridge leading into City Island – could this sleepy hamlet of wood-shingled buildings and antique stores be part of the boogie-down Bronx?

Absolutely! The 'Bronx Riviera' is a beautiful stretch of sand and surf overlooking the Long Island Sound about 20 miles northeast of midtown Manhattan.

Despite the provincial surroundings, life on City Island is pretty sophisticated; it's home to three art galleries, a host of museums and the best seafood restaurants in five boroughs. There are two annual art shows – one in spring and one in fall – but there's no 'right time' to visit. The teardrop shaped Victorian lights illuminating the main drag, the beautiful period architecture along Schofield Street, and the near perpetual morning fog lend the area an anachronistic charm that doesn't lessen with the changing seasons.

INFORMATION
- 🚇 No 6 train to Pelham Bay Park, then bus Bx29 to City Island
- ☎ 718-885-9100 (Chamber of Commerce)
- 💻 www.cityislandchamber.org
- ✖ City Island Diner (☎ 718-885-0808; 304 City Island Ave btwn Fordham and Hawkins Sts)

Dia Center (5, B1)

The Hudson River Valley has entered a new era of hipness thanks to the Dia Center, which has turned an abandoned paper factory in the small town of Beacon into a fabulous museum easily reached in a day. The Riggio Galleries house the Center's impressive permanent collection, including early works by Andy Warhol, monumental sculptures by Richard Serra, a series of fluorescent light pieces by Dan Flavin and several mixed-media installations by Joseph Beuys, as well as many other works.

A 90-minute ride on the Metro-North railway, Beacon enjoys a privileged spot right on the Hudson River and the surrounding nature is as magnificent as anything on display inside the museum. The Dia Center is still working on the exteriors and has plans to expand its galleries throughout 90 acres of adjacent riverfront land.

INFORMATION
- ☎ 845-440-0100
- 💻 www.diaart.org
- ✉ 3 Beekman St, Beacon, NY
- 💲 $10/7
- 🕑 11am-6pm Thu-Mon, April 15-Oct 18; 11am-4pm Fri-Mon Oct 18-Apr 15
- 🚆 Metro-North train, Hudson Valley Line from Grand Central Terminal, and 5-min walk to museum; a trolley runs the 'Loop' from Dia to Main St and train station on weekends
- ♿ Wheelchair accessible, wheelchairs available on site
- ✖ Snacks and lunches, organic beverages from local farms

Fire Island, NY (5, B2)

This idyllic setting is enhanced by a lack of traffic jams and exhaust fumes – car access is limited on this tranquil little place off Long Island. Its 26 miles (42km) of beaches are easily traversed by bike and there are plenty of tiny villages in which to dine and shop. The **Fire Island National Seashore** (☎ 631-289-4810; www.nps.gov/fiis/) has a number of visitors centers set up around

INFORMATION
☎ 718-217-5477 (Long Island Rail Road)
🖳 www.mta.nyc.ny.us/lirr

the island to provide information on camping, boating, kayaking and other nature programs, and to help people access the impressive sand dunes. There are ranger-led tours of the Sailors Haven (aka Sunken Forest) and other attractions. At night, people head to Cherry Grove or the Pines for some fun – these two gay communities are within walking distance of each other and are famous for all-night dance parties open to all.

Sandy Hook, NJ (5, A2)

When you are most in need of a beach break, the New York Waterway Ferry comes through – hop on a ferry at W 38th (3, A1) or the World Financial Center (3, C8) and head to Sandy Hook, part of New Jersey's stunning Gateway National Recreation Area. The 60-minute ferry ride is a nice way to start (and end) a day at the beach, taking you slowly underneath the Verrazano-Narrows Bridge and dropping you at the historic Fort Hancock army base. From there, yellow buses drop you off at any of six great beaches. Each has cabanas

INFORMATION
☎ 800-53-FERRY (New York Waterway Ferry)
🖳 www.nywaterway.com
✉ Pier 78 at W 38th St or World Financial Center
$ Round-trip tickets $27/13
🕑 weekend mornings

for changing, snacks for munching and plenty of sunshine. **New Jersey Transit** (☎ 973-762-5100; www.njtransit.com) also has trains that go to Sandy Hook and other places along the Jersey shore – it takes about 90 minutes from Manhattan.

ORGANIZED TOURS

It's not hard to find good tour guides in New York – most locals think they know enough to fit the bill! Here's a run down of the best in town.

Atlantic Kayak Tours New York (4, A2) Kayak tours through Manhattan Harbor yield grand views of the city. Other advanced tours go from Staten Island to Coney Island; Staten Island to Sandy Hook; and around Manhattan.
☎ 845-246-2187
💻 www.atlantickay aktours.com ✉ tours depart Liberty State Park in Jersey City, NJ
💲 advanced tours $50, equipment hire $45

Big Apple Jazz Tours (6, A2) These tours give music fans an opportunity to see Manhattan's jazz scene from the inside, including a chance to jam with the big boys. Fabulously informative and entertaining, even aficionados will be impressed.
☎ 212-304-8186
💻 www.bigapplejazz .com ✉ 3268 43rd St, Long Island City, Queens
💲 $50-100 ⌚ tour times vary

Big Onion Walking Tours (6, A4) Tours of all types, led by local professors. The Gangland tour is quite popular, and if you're a foodie the multi-ethnic eating tour shouldn't be missed.
☎ 212-439-1090
💻 www.bigonion.com
✉ 476 13th St, Brooklyn NY 💲 $12/10 ⌚ Tours Fri & Sat Sep-May, Wed-Sun summer

The jet set wouldn't tour Manhattan any other way

Bike Big Apple Fabulous, informative tours on two wheels through all sorts of ethnic 'nabes and historic enclaves, all biking skill levels are welcome. Tours change regularly but all are professionally run and quite fun. Year round, too!
☎ 201-837-1133
💻 www.bikethebigapple .com 💲 4hr tour $59

Circle Line Tours (2, A8) Making a complete circle around Manhattan (hence the name), these boat tours provide glimpses of all five boroughs as well as fantastic views of many New York sights.
☎ 212-563-3200
💻 www.circleline42 .com ✉ Pier 83 W 42nd St 💲 depending on tour $12-39

Gray Line New York Sightseeing (2, B8) Double-decker buses do the signature city loop, allowing you to jump on and off at will when something really catches your fancy. Tons of other tours also available, like the Harlem Gospel Tour.
☎ 212-445-0848
💻 www.graylinenew york.com ✉ Eighth Ave 42nd St Port Authority Terminal 💲 tours $37-89
⌚ 8am-midnight

Harlem Heritage Tours All the fabulous culture of Harlem is on display in these tours – Spanish Harlem, Malcolm X's Harlem, the Renaissance of Harlem, soul food and jazz tours too.
☎ 212-280-7888
💻 www.harlemheritage .com ✉ Ste 5C, 230 W 116th St 💲 depending on tour $20-60 ⌚ tour times vary

Helicopter Flight Services (3, D9) Get a bird's eye view of all your favorite Manhattan locations on these whirlwind tours of the island, even going all the way up to Yankee Stadium.
☎ 212-355-0801
💻 www.heliny.com
✉ Downtown Heliport Pier 6 💲 $109-159

The kayak guide who got away

☎ 212-613-5796
✉ White Horse Tavern, 567 Hudson St $ $12
☉ 2pm Sat

New York Waterways (3, A1) Two-hour tours, 90 minute tours, Twilight and Friday Night Dancing Cruises, as well as full-day Hudson trips are offered by NY Waterways. New tours are always in the pipeline; it has great diversity.
☎ 800-533-3779
💻 www.nywaterway .com ✉ Pier 78 on W 38th St & other city locations $ depending on tour $12-49

☉ 10am-6pm Mon-Fri, 11am-6pm Sat & Sun

A Hip Hop Look at New York from Hush Tours Led by hip hop artists, these tours are fascinating glimpses into an art form and a culture. Tours include stops in the Bronx, Harlem, Brooklyn and Lower East Side.
☎ 212-714-3527
💻 www.hushtours.com ✉ 292 Fifth Ave $ 4hrtours $75 ☉ 1 Sat a month winter, twice a month summer, private tours on request

Manhattan Kayak (3, A2) Great kayak tours all around Manhattan, through the downtown harbor to see the Statue of Liberty, as well as trips out to Coney Island, Staten Island and New Jersey.
☎ 212-924-1788
💻 www.manhat tankayak.com ✉ Pier 63 at W 23rd St & Hudson River $ tours $75, 3.5hr lesson $150 ☉ 11am-7pm

Literary Pub Crawls (3, B4) Feed your artistic side with an inspiring tour of the West Village's many writerly haunts, often conveniently located in neighborhood pubs. Guides read from associated works while you soak up the culture (and some brews). Reservations (through the New Ensemble Theater Co) are suggested.

Tightwad Treks (6, B4) These guides know where big bargains can be found, and they are willing to share their expertise. The Elegant Tightwad also does upscale shopping tours, garment district tours, and many other bargain-hunting excursions.
☎ 631-841-2111
💻 www.theelegant tightwad.com ✉ 282 New York Ave, Huntington, NY $ per person $55-99

Free Tours
Take a tour of fabulous **Grand Central Terminal** with the **Municipal Art Society** (☎ 212-935-3960; www.mas.org; $ suggested donation; ☉ 12:30pm Wed). There are also free tours of New York's fascinating neighborhoods, including historic **34th St** with the **34th St Partnership** (☎ 212-719-3434; www.34th Street.org), a grand tour of Midtown with the **Grand Central Partnership** (☎ 212-883-2420; www.grandcentralpartnership.org) or a tour of Times Sq with the **Times Sq Alliance** (☎ 212-768-1560; timessquarebid.org). On Saturdays, the **14th Street-Union Sq Business Improvement District** (☎ 212-460-1204; www.unionsquarenyc.org; ☉ 2pm) runs a free walking tour through the Union Sq area. It includes stops at New York's first film studios, opera houses, grand theaters and nickelodeons, 'Ladies' Mile' and Union Sq Park.

Shopping

Funky couture shops and sleek designer stores beguile you with dashing window displays; mammoth megastores in Times Sq and beyond brashly call for your attention; and all over the city, no matter what the product, merchants stand ready to convince you that yes, they have what you want and yes, you need what they have.

Stores are generally open between 10am and 8pm daily, except Lower Manhattan (which tends to close up on weekends) and establishments run by Orthodox Jews (closed Saturdays). Expect a hefty sales tax of 8.25% unless it's 'tax-free week', usually in August, when all clothing purchases under $500 are tax exempt. End-of-summer 'mini-sales' help whip the shopping public into a frenzy, and prices also fall precipitously in January and early July, when Barneys and Saks have legendary sales. With so many stores to choose from, there's always a bargain to be had; check NY Sale (www.nysale.com) or Lazar Shopping (www.lazarshopping.com).

Neighborhoods and trends shift pretty quickly but as a general rule Madison Ave and the Upper East Side have the big-name designer brands; fresh looks for the eternally hip can be found in Soho and Nolita; funky boutiques and music shops reside in the East Village; and Greenwich Village offers an eclectic mix of high-end and offbeat clothing and antique stores. For fun and flashy souvenirs head to Chinatown, South St Seaport or Times Sq.

Top Five Streets for Shopping
- Fifth Ave from 42nd St to Central Park Sth
- Madison Ave from 50th to 57th Sts
- Bleecker St in Greenwich Village
- West Broadway & Prince Sts in Soho
- Mott St from Nolita to Chinatown

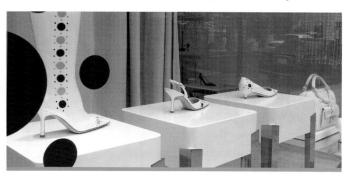

DEPARTMENT STORES

Barneys (2, D6) Barneys has spot-on collections of designer clothes (Marc Jacobs, Prada, Helmut Lang, Paul Smith, Miu Miu shoes etc). Less expensive deals (geared a bit younger) are at Co-Op Barneys on the 7th and 8th floors, or in Chelsea or Soho. Warehouse sales are held in February and August.
☎ 212-826-8900
💻 www.barneys.com
✉ 660 Madison Ave
🕐 10am-8pm Mon-Fri, 10am-7pm Sat, 11am-6pm Sun ⊖ N, R, W to Fifth Ave/59th St

Bergdorf Goodman (2, D7) Dripping elegance from every floor, Bergdorf Goodman is known for terrific jewelry and couture collections, as well as attentive staff who seem genuinely friendly. The men's collection is across Fifth Ave at 745 Fifth Ave.
☎ 212-753-7300
💻 http://bergdorfgoodman.com ✉ 754 Fifth Ave 🕐 10am-7pm Mon-Wed & Fri,

10am-8pm Thu, noon-8pm Sun ⊖ N, R, W to Fifth Ave, F to 57th St

Bloomingdale's (2, D7) Massive 'Bloomies' is historic, sprawling and overwhelming but you don't want to miss it. Its unmistakable 'brown bags' pepper the streets of Manhattan, but the store is also known for great clothing and shoes from a who's-who of designers, including an increasing number of just-off-the-runway collections.
☎ 212-705-2000
💻 www.bloomingdales.com ✉ 1000 Third Ave at 59th St 🕐 10am-8:30pm Mon-Thu, 9am-10pm Fri & Sat, 11am-7pm Sun ⊖ 4, 5, 6 to 59th St, N, R, W to Lexington Ave/59th St

H&M (2, C9) The flagship store in Herald Sq is hugely popular with young shoppers and you'll find the occasional hipster cruising the aisles as well. The Swedish knock-off chain has five other locations in New

York, but this is the biggest and best one.
☎ 646-473-1164
💻 www.hm.com
✉ 1328 Broadway at 34th St 🕐 10am-10pm Mon-Sat, 11am-8pm Sun ⊖ B, D, F, N, Q, R, V, W to 34th St/Herald Sq

Henri Bendel (2, D7) A big-name, high-class department store, Bendel's makes for a cozy pop in and out. Lots of curious, stylish clothing from established and newly-arrived designers, as well as cosmetics and accessories. The windows are also worth looking at.
☎ 212-247-1100
💻 www.henribendel.com ✉ 712 Fifth Ave 🕐 10am-7pm Fri-Wed, 10am-8pm Thu ⊖ E, V to Fifth Ave/53rd St or N, R, W to Fifth Ave/59th St

Loehmann's (3, B3) A good place to save cash while picking up some downscaled designer clothes, Loehmann's gets a pretty diverse crowd, spread out through five stories of mostly moderately priced products.
☎ 212-352-0856
💻 www.loehmanns.com ✉ 101 Seventh Ave at 16th St 🕐 9am-9pm Mon-Sat, 11am-7pm Sun ⊖ 1, 9 to 18th St

Lord & Taylor (2, D9) A gleaming department store filled with classic American designers, from Ralph Lauren to Calvin Klein, Lord & Taylor has marvelous casual wear and

Hanging out at Pearl River Mart

great watches, jewelry, cosmetics and kids clothes.
☎ 212-391-3344
💻 www.lordandtaylor.com ✉ 424 Fifth Ave
🕐 10am-8:30pm Mon-Fri, 10am-7pm Sat, 11am-7pm Sun 🚇 6 to 33rd St, 7 to Fifth Ave, S, 4, 5, 6, 7 to Grand Central/42nd St

Macy's (2, C9) It claims to be the world's largest department store, although there's never been any hard data offered as proof. In any case, it's a massive old store with lots of quirky touches (rickety elevators) that have earned New Yorkers' affection. You won't find the up-to-the-minute fashions here but lots of solid classics.
☎ 212-695-4400
💻 www.macys.com ✉ 151 W 34th St at Broadway 🕐 10am-8:30pm Mon-Sat, 11am-7pm Sun 🚇 B, D, F, N, Q, R, V, W to 34th St/Herald Sq

Pearl River Mart (3, C6) Spread across two floors, Pearl River Mart stocks amazing Asian ceramics, kitchenware, art and traditional clothing and accessories (particularly women's brocade gowns and robes). Choose from a variety of sake sets, or purchase a Japanese Sumi brush and start a new hobby. Prices are terrific – if you can find these items uptown, you'll pay twice the amount.
☎ 212-431-4770
💻 www.pearlriver.com ✉ 477 Broadway 🕐 10am-7pm 🚇 J, M, N, Q, R, W, Z, 6 to Canal St

Ralph Lauren (2, D5) Ralph Lauren's flagship store is in a beautiful 1890s mansion that makes the long trek up Madison Ave worthwhile. There's a large selection of all types of clothes in the traditional Polo style, with emphasis on formal wear, particularly for men.
☎ 212-606-2100
💻 www.polo.com ✉ 867 Madison Ave 🕐 10am-6pm Mon-Wed & Fri, 10am-7pm Thu, noon-5pm Sun 🚇 6 to 68th St/Hunter College

Saks Fifth Avenue (2, D8) Now an ubiquitous presence around the city, the Saks flagship space features an updated and elegant collection of high-end women's and men's clothing. The January sale is a favorite among New Yorkers, who also come for the stellar Rockefeller Center views.
☎ 212-753-4000
💻 www.saksfifthavenue.com ✉ 611 Fifth Ave at 50th St 🕐 10am-7pm Mon-Wed, Fri & Sat, 10am-8pm Thu, noon-6pm Sun 🚇 B, D, F, V to 47-50th Sts

Takashimaya (2, D7) Takashimaya's gorgeous signature packages can be spotted all over town; New Yorkers have embraced the minimalist ethos at this elegant uptown store. Lovely house wares and other goods from around the world are the store specialty, but even if you don't buy anything, you can still stop for tea in the basement Teabox.
☎ 212-350-0100
💻 www.takashimaya.com ✉ 693 Fifth Ave 🕐 10am-7pm Mon-Sat, noon-5pm Sun 🚇 E, V to Fifth Ave/53rd St

Century 21

When this New York institution finally reopened its doors a few months after the World Trade Center tragedy, a wave of relief swept across the city. It's everybody's favorite place for deep discounts on designer clothing, accessories, shoes and perfume – sometimes more than half off the original price. (3, C8; ☎ 212-227-9092; 22 Cortland St at Church St; 🕐 7:45am-8pm Mon-Wed & Fri, 7:45am-8:30pm Thur, 10am-8pm Sat, 11am-7pm Sun; A, C, 4, 5 to Fulton St-Broadway Nassau)

FASHION & COUTURE

Always ready to defend its self-appointed title of fashion capital of the world, New York now has a new weapon in the fight for shopping supremacy – the downtown 'co-op' store that has all the cachet of uptown flagships but slightly lower prices. Many big names – Ralph Lauren, Armani, Gucci etc – have proudly set up satellites in Soho.

Calvin Klein (2, D6)
Always upping the ante, Calvin Klein has made unstudied elegance a look, a lifestyle – maybe even an art – and it's all on display in this gorgeous store. The signature casual clothes sit next to more formal designs that are equally entrancing.
☎ 212-292-9000
💻 www.calvinklein.com
✉ 654 Madison Ave
🕐 10am-6pm Mon-Wed, Fri & Sat, 10am-7pm Sat, noon-6pm ⊕ 4, 5, 6 to 59th St

Donna Karan (2, D6)
Clean lines, attractive details, understated yet sexy colors have made Donna Karan's clothes and accessories absolutely indispensable to busy career women in New York and beyond. The gorgeous Madison Ave store is almost like a spa, it's so refreshing to visit.
☎ 866-240-4700
💻 www.donnakaran .com ✉ 819 Madison Ave
🕐 10am-6pm Mon-Wed, Fri & Sat, 10am-7pm Thu
⊕ 6 to 68th St-Hunter College

Givenchy (2, D6) Located in a fabulous freestanding boutique, Givenchy New York carries sharkskin power suits, floaty ball gowns, a full line of daywear, bags, perfumes, creams and accessories. Plus, the in-house tailor is considered the best in town.
☎ 212-772-1040
💻 www.givenchy.fr
✉ 710 Madison Ave
🕐 10am-6pm Mon-Wed, Fri & Sat, 10am-7pm Thu, noon-6pm Sun ⊕ N, R, W to Fifth Ave-59th St, 4, 5, 6 to 59th St

Gucci (2, D7) Five stories of super luxurious ready-to-wear clothing have earned Gucci a loyal clientele. All the classics are available, including stylish Gucci handbags and high-heeled shoes, as well as new and modern looks right off the rack.
☎ 212-826-2600
💻 www.gucci.com
✉ 685 Fifth Ave
🕐 10am-6:30pm Mon-Fri, 10am-7pm Sat, noon-6pm Sun ⊕ E, V to Fifth Ave/53rd St

Helmut Lang (3, C5) Sleek and unobtrusive, Helmut Lang's flagship store features

CLOTHING & SHOE SIZES

Women's Clothing

Aust/UK	8	10	12	14	16	18
Europe	36	38	40	42	44	46
Japan	5	7	9	11	13	15
USA	6	8	10	12	14	16

Women's Shoes

Aust/USA	5	6	7	8	9	10
Europe	35	36	37	38	39	40
France only	35	36	38	39	40	42
Japan	22	23	24	25	26	27
UK	3½	4½	5½	6½	7½	8½

Men's Clothing

Aust	92	96	100	104	108	112
Europe	46	48	50	52	54	56

Japan	S	M	M		L	
UK/USA	35	36	37	38	39	40

Men's Shirts (Collar Sizes)

Aust/Japan	38	39	40	41	42	43
Europe	38	39	40	41	42	43
UK/USA	15	15½	16	16½	17	17½

Men's Shoes

Aust/ UK	7	8	9	10	11	12
Europe	41	42	43	44½	46	47
Japan	26	27	27.5	28	29	30
USA	7½	8½	9½	10½	11½	12½

Measurements approximate only; try before you buy.

the very latest in urban chic with its own ready-to-wear collection. Simple-looking clothes always have some kind of hidden luxury tucked away – Lang's genius is in the detail.

☎ 212-925-7214
💻 www.helmutlang.com
✉ 80 Greene St
🕑 11am-7pm Mon-Sat, noon-6pm Sun ⊙ N, R, W to Prince St, 6 to Spring St

Prada's army

Jeffrey New York (3, B3)
An early arrival to the Meat-packing District, Jeffrey New York has definitely classed up the 'hood. The store sells high-end designer clothing and accessories in a roomy modern space with an outstanding shoe selection (Prada, Gucci, etc.).

☎ 212-206-1272
💻 www.jeffreynewyork .com ✉ 449 W 14th St
🕑 10am-8pm Mon-Wed & Fri, 10am-9pm Thu, 10am-7pm Sat, 12:30-6pm Sun ⊙ A, C, E to 14th St, L to Eighth Ave

Kirna Zabete (3, C5)
Everybody loves Kirna Zabete for its glam clothing (Balenciaga, Jean Paul Gaultier, Alice Roi) but people return because of the professional and friendly service, as well as the fun setting. Besides clothes you get perfume, watches, shoes and you can even check your email while you shop!

☎ 212-941-9656
💻 www.kirnazabete .com ✉ 96 Greene St
🕑 11am-7pm Mon-Sat, noon-6pm Sun ⊙ N, R to Prince St

Luca Luca (2, D6)
Every A-list party girl has to have at least one Luca Luca item in her closet – and even if you don't frequent red carpets, you should have one too. Luxurious and feminine are the watchwords at this store and you are allowed (encouraged even!) to take your time browsing. Staff members offer espresso coffees between try-ons.

☎ 212-753-2444
💻 www.lucaluca.org
✉ 690 Madison Ave
🕑 11am-6:30pm Mon-Wed & Sat, 11am-8pm Thu ⊙ N, R, W to Fifth Ave/59th St, 4, 5, 6 to 59th St

Marc Jacobs (3, B4)
This one block on Bleecker St should be renamed now that Marc Jacobs has turned three huge storefronts into his own personal property. Gorgeous leather bags and accessories at No 385, men's apparel at No 403 and women get a store of their own at No 405.

☎ 212-924-0026
💻 www.marcjacobs.com
✉ 403, 405 Bleecker St; accessories: 385 Bleecker St 🕑 noon-8pm Mon-Sat, noon-7pm Sun ⊙ 1, 9 to Christopher St-Sheridan Sq

Prada (2, D7)
A perennial favorite among New Yorkers, Prada's elegant designs and sensuous materials are as recognizable as the Empire State Building. The flagship store on Fifth Ave has fine Italian clothing for men and women while shoes are sold at 45 E 57th St.

☎ 212-664-0010
💻 www.prada.com
✉ 724 Fifth Ave
🕑 10am-6pm Mon-Wed, Fri & Sat, noon-6pm Sun ⊙ N, R, W to Fifth Ave/59th St

Valentino (2, D6)
If you like your clothes to get more attention that you do, Valentino's sexy, swaggering styles are just for you. Gorgeous Italian designs make the most of the human body and seem to hang just right, no matter what your measurements. Lots of bright colors and ruffled necklines (ruffled plunging necklines, that is) are featured.

☎ 212-772-6969
💻 www.valentino.it
✉ 747 Madison Ave
🕑 10am-6pm Mon-Wed, Fri & Sat, 10am-7pm Thu ⊙ F to Lexington Av/63rd St

SHOES, JEWELRY & ACCESSORIES

Shoes

Jimmy Choo (2, D7)
These shoes are gorgeous. Magnificent. Really. Not many things can live up to the hype, especially the hype around these shoes, but Jimmy Choo delivers.
☎ 212-593-0800
🖳 www.jimmychoo.com
✉ 645 Fifth Ave at 51st St ⏲ 10am-6pm Mon-Sat, noon-5pm Sun
Ⓔ E, V to Fifth Ave-53rd St, 6 to 51st St

John Fleuvog (3, D5)
Funky thick-soled shoes can still have a great heel, as shown in this sexy collection. These ever-funky, ever-urban shoes with trademark two-tone arrow stitches have universal appeal.
☎ 212-431-4484
🖳 www.fluevog.com
✉ 250 Mulberry St
⏲ noon-8pm Mon-Sat, noon-6pm Sun Ⓔ 6 to Spring St, N, R to Prince St

Jewelry

Borealis (3, D5) This tiny store packs in a wide variety of styles and prices. Earrings are particularly entrancing, with delicate Asian designs contrasting with large, jewel-studded Brazilian pieces.
☎ 917-237-0152 ✉ 229 Elizabeth St ⏲ noon-7pm Mon-Sat, 1-6pm Sun
Ⓔ 6 to Bleecker St

Cartier (2, D7) Engagement rings and wedding bands of contemporary design make up Cartier's aptly named Love collection. Or there's the signature gold Trinity rings and classic watches for men on offer.
☎ 212-446-3459
🖳 www.cartier.com
✉ 653 Fifth Ave near 52nd St ⏲ 10am-5:30pm Mon-Sat, noon-5pm Sun
Ⓔ N, R, E, F to Fifth Ave, B, V to 57th St

Tenthousandthings (3, B3) Understated jewels that nonetheless stand out are the specialty of this popular store, which combines unique metals with eye-catching stones and settings for a one-of-a-kind look.
☎ 212-352-1333
🖳 www.tenthousand
things.com ✉ 423 W 14th St ⏲ noon-6pm Mon-Fri Ⓔ 1, 9 to 14th St

Tiffany & Co (2, D7) Oh, the cachet of that little blue box! Tiffany's signature packaging is recognized the world over, and whether you're sporting one of the store's classic six-prong diamond rings or a Tiffany key ring, a visit here is always something special.
☎ 212-755-8000
🖳 www.tiffany.com
✉ 727 Fifth Ave at 57th St ⏲ 10am-6pm Mon-Fri, 10am-6pm Sat, noon-5pm Sun Ⓔ N, R to Fifth Ave, E, F to Fifth Ave, V to 57th St

Accessories

Cobblestones (3, D4) That vintage Hermès scarf you've longed for all your life? It may be here. Want some Jackie O pillbox hats for your retro look? This is the place. Space is tight – the changing room is a screen against the wall.
☎ 212-673-5372 ✉ 314 E 9th St ⏲ 1-7pm Tue-Sun Ⓔ 6 to Astor Pl

Kate Spade (3, C6) Still going strong years after being dubbed Manhattan's 'It' girl, Kate Spade's handbags, sunglasses and various accoutrements are de rigueur for really put-together urbanites. Newly launched collections include baby gear and home furnishings.
☎ 212-274-1991
🖳 www.katespade.com
✉ 454 Broome St
⏲ 11am-7pm Mon-Sat, noon-6pm Sun Ⓔ N, R, W to Prince St, 6 to Spring St

Quick Boutique Peeks
Local designers with loyal followings include:
- **Catherine** (3, C6; ☎ 212-925-6765; 468 Broome St) Party dresses and frocks
- **Kleins of Monticello** (3, E5; ☎ 212-966-1453; 105 Orchard St) Affordable chic
- **A Cheng** (3, E4; ☎ 212-979-7324; 443 E 9th St) An East Village fave
- **Nellie M** (2, D4; ☎ 212-996-4410; 1309 Lexington Ave) Fresh work from new designers

ARTS & ANTIQUES

Antiquarium (2, D5) This gallery features glamorous, very wearable antique Classical and Near Eastern jewelry from around the world. Earrings look like Cleopatra just took them off, and if you've been eyeing the Egyptian sarcophagi at the Met, this is where you get one for yourself.
☎ 212-734-9776 ✉ 948 Madison Ave ⏰ 10am-5:30pm Tue-Sat; shorter hrs in summer Ⓜ 6 to 77th St-Lexington Ave

Art & Tapisserie (2, D3) Great for kids, this store is crammed full with toys, including popular items like rocking chairs, antique piggy banks, hooded towels, toy chests, Madeline collectible clothing and Teletubbies. The store's costume section offers sequined dresses and boas too. And Art & Tapisserie's talented staff will personalize just about anything with beautiful calligraphy or paintings and images.
☎ 212-722-3222 ✉ 1242 Madison Ave near 89th St ⏰ 10:30am-6:30pm Mon-Fri, 10am-6pm Sat, noon-5pm Sun Ⓜ 4, 5, 6 to 86th St

Bernard & S Dean Levy (2, D4) The Levys' expansive collection of American antiques and art includes lots of mirrors. An American Girondole mirror with four candle arms and a black eagle is the pride of the showroom. A few European pieces are here too – a Queen Anne Chippendale

mirror is on the 2nd floor of the five-floor emporium.
☎ 212-628-7088 ⌨ www.levygalleries .com ✉ 24 E 84th St at Madison Ave ⏰ 9:30am-5:30pm Tue-Sat, open Mon as well Ⓜ 4, 5, 6 to 86th St

Fanelli Antique Timepieces (2, D6) Clocks that have been handed down for generations are brought here when they need repairs. Sotheby's and Tiffany send their own engineers here for training and advice. There are clocks with unique histories, like the maritime clocks, and others that graced the walls of famous houses. Plenty of gorgeous investment pieces are available.
☎ 212-517-2300 ✉ 790 Madison Ave near 67th St ⏰ 9am-6pm Mon-Fri, 11am-6pm Sat from Oct-May Ⓜ 6 to 68th St-Hunter College

Gallery of Wearable Art (2, D6) Lots of big Hollywood names have unique, one-of-a-kind clothes from here, many featuring appliqués picked out by an in-house designer in consultation with clients. Custom-made bridal and mother-of-the-bride dresses are a specialty.
☎ 212-570-2252 ⌨ www.galleryofwear ableart.com ✉ 34 E 67th St ⏰ call for an appointment Ⓜ 6 to 68th St-Hunter College

Manhattan Art & Antique Center (2, E7) This Midtown counterpart to the Chelsea

antique industry is home to 100 galleries selling just about any kind of antique tapestries, paintings, jewelry, and furnishings you can imagine. Many of the vendors will repair your old stuff, too. Beautiful rugs can be found here, many brought over from Turkey and Pakistan.
☎ 212-355-4400 ⌨ www.the-maac.com ✉ 1050 Second Ave at 55th St ⏰ 10:30am-6pm Mon-Sat, noon-6pm, individual galleries may have different hrs Ⓜ N, R, 4, 5, 6 to 59th St-Lexington Ave

Martin Lane Historical Americana (3, C5) This dealer specializes in antique Colt firearms but collectors can find almost anything military here, at all price levels. A few years back, owner Martin Lane got hold of an 1875 Remington that belonged to Jesse James, which he then sold for $400,000.
☎ 212-206-1004 ⌨ www.historyonhand .com ✉ 205 W Houston St ⏰ call for appointment Ⓜ 1, 9 to Houston

Philip Colleck (2, E7) The location of this store – a pre-Civil War landmark brick house – is worth checking out, along with the collection of William & Mary, Queen Anne, Georgian, Chippendale, Hepplewhite, Sheraton and Regency furniture, with an emphasis on chinoiserie, mirrors and screens.
☎ 212-505-2500
🖳 www.philipcolleck .com ✉ 311 E 58th St
🕒 11am-6pm Mon-Fri
🚇 N, R, 4, 5, 6 to 59th St-Lexington Ave

Remains Antique Lighting (3, C2) Formerly an architectural salvage shop, this big store now has dozens of different lights – some old, some new – and offers free wiring to local residents with purchases. The inverted-dome chandeliers and stellar sconces end up gracing some of the most celebrated city habitats, as well as many a movie set.
☎ 212-675-8051
🖳 www.remains.com

✉ 130 W 28th St
🕒 9am-6pm Mon-Fri, 11am-6pm Sat 🚇 1, 9 to 23rd St

Stardust Antiques (3, D3) A rambling, eclectic shop with enchanting rooms, Stardust Antiques has myriad paintings, furnishings and accessories. It's particularly known around town for its for early 19th century, Edwardian and Art Deco wedding bands and engagement rings.
☎ 212-677-2590
🖳 www.stardust antiques.com ✉ 38 Gramercy Park, 21st St near Park Ave 🕒 noon-7pm Mon-Sat, noon-6pm Sun 🚇 N, R, 6 to 23rd St

Susan Parrish Antiques (3, B4) American furniture, textiles, folk art and paintings are offered at this well-respected West Village antiques store. There are early 20th century Amish quilts and furnishings, as well as 19th century items in

good condition. Navajo and hooked rugs come in dozens of floral and geometric designs.
☎ 212-645-5020 ✉ 390 Bleecker St 🕒 noon-7pm Mon-Sat (or by appointment) 🚇 1, 9 to Christopher St-Sheridan Sq

Sylvia Pines Uniquities (2, D5) All the pretty Victorian, French and Art Deco handbags in this vintage jewelry shop are handmade – many on sterling-silver frames or with semiprecious-stone accents. The staff can repair small snags in one of your own bags, but it's next to impossible to leave without buying something!
☎ 212-744-5141
✉ 1102 Lexington Ave 🕒 10am-5pm Mon-Fri in summer, 10am-5pm Mon-Sat in winter 🚇 6 to 77th St-Lexington Ave

Triple Pier Antique Show (2, A7) This massive show has more than 600 dealers of old furniture, collectibles, clothing and a range of other treasures. Stores stock up here, decorators come to get ideas, and regular shoppers go berserk in this antiquing haven. The Americana section can turn up surprising bargains. The show is held annually over two consecutive weekends in November – check the website for dates.
☎ 212-255-0020
🖳 www.stellashows .com ✉ Twelfth Ave btwn 48th & 55th Sts
🕒 11am-6pm Sat & Sun 🚇 A, B, C, D, 1, 9 to 59th St

Antiquing Chelsea

It's down from six parking lots to two, but dealers and decorators still vie for the good stuff at the **Annex Antique Fair & Flea Market** (3, C2; ☎ 212-243-5343 ✉ 107-111 W 25th St 💲 entry $1 🕒 dawn-dusk Sat & Sun 🚇 F, V, 1, 9 to 23rd St). If you want to work it like a pro come early (5am) with a flashlight, and shop off the trucks. Spillover flea markets abound on weekends, with two big free ones at Sixth Ave and 24th St.

Or you could try the **Garage Antique Fair** (3, C2; ☎ 212-647-0707 ✉ 112 W 25th St 🕒 dawn-dusk Sat & Sun 🚇 F, V, 1, 9 to 23rd St). Two levels in this covered parking lot are turned over to 150 vendors on weekends and it's a great place to browse. Plenty of old photos, posters and assorted furnishings.

MUSIC & BOOKS

Bobby's Happy House (1, C2) Part of Harlem history, Bobby's specializes in deep gospel sounds. The owner, Bobby Robinson, worked with Elmore James and produced Gladys Knight & the Pips, whom he also named. The store has R&B, blues and just a few funk albums to go along with the gospel.
☎ 212-663-5240
✉ 2335 Fred Douglas Blvd ⏲ 11am-8pm daily ⊕ A, C, B or D to 125th-St. Nicholas Ave

Books of Wonder (3, C3) Kids who love to read (or be read to) will love this cozy haven. Welcoming staff allow visitors to roam and touch at will, and even the rare editions can be pulled off shelves and perused (albeit with supervision).
☎ 212-989-3270
🖥 www.booksofwonder .com ✉ 16 W 18th St ⏲ 11am-7pm Mon-Sat, 11:45am-6pm Sun ⊕ L, N, R, 4, 5, 6 to Union Sq

Colony (2, C8) Charlie Parker and Miles Davis bought their sheet music here. Colony's collection of tunes remains the city's largest; there are also karaoke CDs, and tons of memorabilia from the Beatles, Frank Sinatra, Tony Bennett, and more.
☎ 212-265-2050
🖥 www.colonymusic .com ✉ 1619 Broadway ⏲ 9:30am-midnight Mon-Sat, 10am-midnight Sun ⊕ 1, 9 to 50th St

etherea (3, D4) etherea carries a particularly good

St Mark's Bookshop: where worlds (and shelves) collide

selection of indie rock, plus some electronica and techno, on both CD and vinyl. The airy space is a welcome respite after a day of browsing – and sneezing – in the dingier shops of the East Village and the Lower East Side.
☎ 212-358-1126
🖥 www.ethereaonline .com ✉ 66 Ave A near 5th St ⏲ noon-10pm Sun-Thu, noon-11pm Fri & Sat ⊕ F to Second Ave

Manny's (2, C8) Manny's sells musical instruments and not music, but if you take your licks seriously, you'll want to see where Jimi Hendrix had his (right-handed) Stratocasters re-strung. Everyone from Dizzy Gillespie to the Beatles has shopped here, leaving behind pictures to prove it.
☎ 212-819-0576
🖥 www.mannysmusic .com ✉ 156 W 48th St ⏲ 10am-7pm Mon-Sat, noon-6pm Sun ⊕ N, R, W to 49th St

Metropolitan Opera Shop (2, B6) Only a lucky few got to hear Renee Fleming's debut performance as

Violetta in La Traviata at the Met, but if a DVD will suffice, this is the spot to get it. The shop has recordings of nearly every song ever sung in opera, and by all the big names. It's a great place for aficionados and neophytes.
☎ 212-580-4090
🖥 www.metguild.org ✉ 136 W 65th St ⏲ 10am-8pm Mon-Sat, noon-6pm Sun ⊕ 1, 9 to 66th St

Oscar Wilde Memorial Bookshop (3, C4) Opened in 1967 this tiny bookstore predates the Stonewall Riot and was an early center of gay and lesbian life in the village. Still geared toward gay and lesbian literature, it also stocks rainbow flags and other gifts.
☎ 212-255-8097
🖥 www.oscarwilde books.com ✉ 15 Christopher St ⏲ 11am-7pm daily ⊕ A, B, C, D, E, F, V to W 4th St, or 1, 9 to Christopher St/Sheridan Sq

St Mark's Bookshop (3, D4) Established in 1977 in the East Village, St Mark's serves a community of

students, academics, arts professionals and other eclectic readers.
☎ 212-260-7853
🖥 www.stmarksbook shop.com ✉ 31 Third Ave ⏱ 10am-midnight Mon-Sat, 11am-midnight Sun ⊕ 6 to Astor Pl

The Strand Bookstore (3, D4) Eight miles of new, used and rare books spread confusingly around one big warehouse-type space. It's a book lover's dream. Another Strand with more room (but less of a range) is on Fulton St in Lower Manhattan.
☎ 212-473-1452
🖥 www.strandbooks .com ✉ 828 Broadway ⏱ 9:30am-10:30pm Mon-Sat, 11am-10:30pm Sun ⊕ L, N, Q, R, W, 4, 5, 6 to 14th St-Union Sq

Three Lives & Co (3, C4) Susan Sontag gave the inaugural reading back in 1978, and since then a steady parade of literati has passed through. Set in an 1830s brick building, the store's burnished-wood bookcases, green-shaded lamps and

old Royal typewriters evoke a bookish gentility. But the books themselves are cutting-edge, which is what keeps discerning readers returning.
☎ 212-741-2069
🖥 www.threelives.com ✉ 154 W 10th St at Waverly Pl ⏱ noon-8pm Mon-Tue, 11am-8:30pm Wed-Sat, noon-7pm Sun ⊕ 1, 2, 3, 9 to 14th St, A, C, E, B, D, F, Q to W 4th St

Used Book Cafe (3, D5) Locals try to keep this place under wraps, as much for its gorgeous spiral staircase and classic library setting as the 45,000 books and CDs lying about at bargain prices. There's a lovely on-site café, and all proceeds benefit Housing Works, a charitable organization serving New York City's HIV-positive and AIDS-afflicted homeless community.
☎ 212-334-3324
🖥 www.housingworks .org ✉ 126 Crosby St ⏱ 10am-9pm Mon-Fri, noon-9pm Sat, noon-7pm Sun ⊕ B, D, F, V to Broadway-Lafayette St

Vinylmania (3, C5) How do New York DJs stay so cuttting edge? Thanks are owed to Vinylmania, where professional spinners stock up on vinyl hip-hop, house, funk and dance music, and a smattering of imported CDs. Remixed versions of popular garage hits also can be found.
☎ 212-924-7223
🖥 www.vinylmania.com ✉ 60 Carmine St ⏱ 11am-8pm Mon-Wed, 11am-9pm Thu-Sat ⊕ A, C, E, B, D, F, Q to W 4th St

Virgin Megastore Times Square (2, C8) This place is swimming with CDs, video games, DVDs, plus 600 listening posts, 100 video viewing stations and more. Adding to the cacophony is the nearby MTV Studios; teen pop stars often drop in for 'impromptu' autograph sessions just as their new CD is being released.
☎ 212-921-1020
🖥 www.virginmega magazine.com ✉ 1540 Broadway ⏱ 9am-1am Sun-Thu, 9am-2am Fri & Sat ⊕ any train to 42nd St-Times Sq

A New York State of Mind

Manhattan has served as a literary backdrop and secondary character in countless novels, essays, and non-fiction works. Here are some books that capture the city's multi-faceted landscapes:

- *The Extra Man* by Jonathan Ames offers an amused look at elegant New York.
- James Baldwin's *Go Tell It On the Mountain* or *Just Above My Head* are masterful works set in the city.
- Anthony Bourdain's *Kitchen Confidential* dishes about the city's best-known chefs.
- Ralph Ellison's *Invisible Man* or the essay 'Harlem is Nowhere' in *Shadow and Act* were precursors to the Harlem Renaissance.
- *Call It Sleep* by Henry Roth is a history of New York Jews.
- Luc Sante's *Low Life* is a fascinating exposé of Lower East Side skullduggery.
- Tom Wolfe's *The Bonfire of the Vanities* is a fictionalized look at city politics.

COMPUTERS & ELECTRONICS

Apple Store Soho (3, C5)
Always busy, this flagship location attracts the full range of computer users – beginners enjoy the translucent stairway and upstairs walkway as much as the cheery-colored iPods, while techheads engage the staff in deep discussions. There's free email service at the store, and seminars on computer tips are also given for free.
☎ 212-226-3126
🖳 www.apple.com/retail/soho ✉ 103 Prince St 🕑 10am-8pm Mon-Sat, 11am-7pm Sun Ⓔ N, R, W to Prince St

B&H Photo-Video (2, B9)
There's simply a bewildering amount of technology and electronics on display at B&H, but since mostly professional photographers and videographers use the store, only the uneducated seem overwhelmed. The establishment is run by Orthodox Jews and it's busy, buzzing and a lot of fun, provided you know what you want and you're not in any hurry.
☎ 212-502-6200
🖳 www.bhphotovideo.com ✉ 420 Ninth Ave 🕑 9am-7pm Mon-Thu, 9am-1pm Fri, 10am-5pm Sun Ⓔ A, C, E to 34th St-Penn Station

Bang & Olufsen (2, D5)
This store has minimalist, upmarket Danish stereo systems that are designed to hang on your wall like art. The BeoSound 2000 CD player opens when you wave your hand near it.

There are several other locations around the city as well.
☎ 212-879-6161
🖳 www.bang-olufsen.com ✉ 952 Madison Ave 🕑 10am-6:30pm Mon-Wed, Fri & Sat, 10am-7pm Thu, noon-5pm Sun Ⓔ 6 to 77th St

Best Buy (3, C3) Despite being a national electronics chain, Best Buy has got some of the most competitive prices in town, especially on a wide range of home-entertainment products, ranging from carousel CD players to plasma-screen TVs. There's also a great DVD selection and tons of bargains to be found in the 'discount' bins in the CD section.
☎ 212-366-1373
🖳 www.bestbuy.com ✉ 60 W 23 St 🕑 10am-9:30pm Mon-Sat, 11am-7pm Sun Ⓔ N, R, 6, 1, 9 to 23rd St

CompUSA (2, D9) Every type of computer or printer accessory you could imagine can be found in CompUSA. The staff are generally helpful although the store gets a bit busy when sales are on. Lots of great computer deals available.
☎ 212-764-6224
🖳 www.compusa.com ✉ 420 Fifth Ave 🕑 8:30am-8pm Mon-Fri, 10am-7pm Sat, 11am-6pm Sun Ⓔ 6 to 42nd St-Grand Central

J&R Music & Computer World (3, D7) Nearly a block-full of shops devoted

The temple of Apple

to cameras, computers, CDs, DVDs, stereos and electronics lines Park Row, each with big selections and sometimes very good deals. Although first started in 1971 as a family-run business, J&R is now a global enterprise with a worldwide reputation.
☎ 212-238-9000
🖳 www.jr.com ✉ 15-23 Park Row 🕑 9am-7:30pm Mon-Sat, 10:30am-6:30pm Sun Ⓔ A, C, J, M, Z, 2, 3, 4, 5 to Fulton St-Broadway Nassau

Tekserve (3, C2) Mac users can't get enough of singing Tekserve's praises. If your computer crashes or you need an estimate on a purchase or you just want to browse among the used and secondhand Macs, this is the best place in town, hands down.
☎ 212-929-3645
🖳 www.tekserve.com ✉ 119 West 23rd Street 🕑 9am-7pm Mon-Fri, 10am-5pm Sat, noon-5pm Sun Ⓔ 1, 9 to 23rd St

FOOD & DRINK

Astor Wines & Spirits

(3, D4) Always a pleasant shopping experience, Astor Wines & Spirits has spacious hardwood aisles full of everything from Beaujolais to Bordeaux. Astor carries a big selection of dessert wines, sake, German wines, and American sparklers. Weekly specials can bring very good wines down to the $10 range.

☎ 212-674-7500

🖳 www.astoruncorked.com ✉ 12 Astor Pl at Lafayette St 🕐 9am-9pm Mon-Sat 🚇 6 to Astor Pl, N, R to 8th St

Chelsea Market (3, B3)

Lots of organic vegetables, homemade cakes, bread, cookies and pies, along with the usual assortment of specialty shops, make the Chelsea Market a hot place to shop (not to mention the free WiFi!). This was once a cookie factory, and the 'fresh-from-the-oven' smell seems baked right in.

☎ 212-243-6005

🖳 www.chelseamarket.com ✉ 75 Ninth Ave btwn W 15th & 16th Sts 🕐 8am-7pm Mon-Sat, 10am-6pm Sun 🚇 1, 9, 2, 3 to 14th St

Whole Foods, whole lotta peppers

Whole Foods Market

(2, C7) This 59,000 sq ft organic supermarket boasts a wine shop, a 248-seat café, a sushi bar, a brick oven, a walk-in greenhouse with fresh flowers, the city's first Jamba Juice, as well as a chocolate store that will put a coat of chocolate on almost anything you want, three hot-food bars (Indian, Latin, Pan-Asian and Chinese), an organic cosmetics center and 49 registers to ring you up. What else could you ever need?

☎ 212-823-9600

🖳 www.wholefoods.com ✉ shops at Columbus Circle, Concourse 1, Broadway btwn 58th & 60th Sts 🕐 8am-10pm 🚇 1, 9, A, C, B, D to 59th St-Columbus Circle

Wild Edibles (2, D8) This

is one of many gourmet food stands in Grand Central Market. The whole market is fantastic, but if you are looking for some jumbo shrimp or fillets of sable, check this stand first. About fifty yards away is Pescatore, another fish stand with excellent specials.

☎ 212-687-4255

🖳 www.grandcentral terminal.com ✉ inside Grand Central Terminal at 42nd St at Lexington Ave 🕐 9am-9pm Mon-Fri, 10am-7pm Sat & Sun 🚇 any train to 42nd St-Grand Central

Zabar's (2, B4) A clas-

sic part of the New York experience, Zabar's serves the freshest, best items. Everybody's favorite place for gelfite fish, whole grain breads and other delectables. It also has a kitchen supply section.

☎ 212-787-2000

🖳 www.zabars.com ✉ 2245 Broadway 🕐 8:30am-7:30pm Mon-Fri, 8am-8pm Sat, 9am-6pm Sun 🚇 1, 9 to 79th St

La Marqueta

Full of flowers, plants, clothes, baskets, dairy products, fresh produce, baked goods, groceries and specialty foods, **La Marqueta** (☎ 212-534-4900 ✉ E 115th St & Park Ave 🕐 9am-6pm 🚇 6 to 116th St/Lexington Ave) is Spanish Harlem's central food market, featuring lots of ethnic products that suit the needs of 'El Barrio.'

FOR CHILDREN

The Children's General Store (2, B3)
This tiny shop has stuffed animals, wind-up toys, costumes and puzzles priced for every budget. A cute touch: it's laid out like a real general store, with dolls and toys stocked as practically as dry goods. Kids will love it. Another store is in Grand Central Terminal, and it's a perfect place to grab something before jumping on a train.
☎ 212-580-2723
✉ 2473 Broadway
☽ 10am-6pm Mon-Fri, 11am-6pm Sat & Sun
Ⓢ 1, 9, 2, 3 to 96th St

Children's Resale (2, E4)
Barely worn apparel for newborns can range from a few dollars for a no-name onesie to significantly more for a Jacadi or Bonpoint outfit. Clothes (up to size 18) are available in a wide range of prices. Most are in great condition; some have suffered a bit of rough-and-tumble.
☎ 212-734-8897
🖳 www.resaleclothing .org ✉ 303 E 81st St
☽ 11am-7pm Mon-Fri, 10am-6pm Sat, noon-5pm Sun Ⓢ 6 to 86th St

Ibiza Kidz (3, C4)
Shoes, shoes, shoes, and an accessory or two. Ibiza is one of those small stores you could spend a good hour browsing in – the toy selection is small but fun, and the clothes are interesting and geared more toward the smallest fashionistas.
☎ 212-533-4614 ✉ 56 University Pl ☽ 11am-

7:30pm Mon-Sat, 12:30-6pm Sun Ⓢ any train to Union Sq

Kimberly Hall Kids (3, C3)
A cool store for kids that aims to make kids' (and parents'!) lives easier with custom designs of everything from bumpers to rockers, supplied from interior designer Hall's giant Rolodex of industry sources. For families who are shopping for a newborn, there is a super-cool Lucite-and-lacquer crib.
☎ 212-254-4006
🖳 www.kimberlyhall kids.com ✉ 44 E 21st St
☽ 10am-6pm Mon-Fri, 11am-6pm Sat & Sun
Ⓢ 6 to 23rd St

Lester's (2, E4)
Moms in the know swear by the wonderful shoe department here, with a selection ranging from casual to dressy. The well-trained staff will fit your son in Nike Prestos and your daughter in Mary Janes. Formalwear includes Perry Ellis and the casual section features Diesel jeans.
☎ 212-734-9292
✉ 1534 Second Ave at 79th St ☽ 10am-6pm Mon-Sat, noon-5pm Sun
Ⓢ 6 to 77th St

Shoofly (2, B4)
Your little one will love these colorful, funky shoes. Look for orange and pink classic patent-leather Mary Janes, D&G junior wrestling boots, and bright suede wallabies from Naturino. Shoofly also

caters for more somber occasions – check out the classic white dress shoes. There's another location in Tribeca on Duane St.
☎ 212-580-4390
🖳 www.shoofynyc.com
✉ 465 Amsterdam Ave
☽ 10am-7pm Mon-Sat, noon-6pm Sun Ⓢ B, C to 81st St, 1, 9 to 79th St

Tigers, Tutus & Toes (3, D4)
This shop stocks whimsical European clothing from designers such as Petit Bateau and Zutano for infants to toddlers. And don't miss the fantastic shoe collection. There's loads of splashy colors and patterns from makers like Keds, Sketchers, and Elefanten in sizes that range from newborn to 10.
☎ 212-228-7990 ✉ 128 Second Ave ☽ 11am-7pm Mon-Sat, noon-6pm Sun Ⓢ 6 to Astor Pl, F to Second Ave

Tod's (2, D7)
There's something for everyone here. Indulgent parents – and grandparents – come here to slip sumptuous suede driving mocs onto precious little piggies. Chic offspring (infants through age 10) can look as stylish as Mom. There are great Diego Della Valle totes for her and sturdy leather shoes for Dad.
☎ 212-644-5945
🖳 www.tods.com
✉ 650 Madison Ave
☽ 10am-6pm Mon-Sat, noon-5pm Sun Ⓢ N, R to Fifth Ave, 4, 5, 6 to 59th St

SPECIALTY STORES

Aedes de Venustas (3, C4)
Step off busy Christopher St and into this plush, inviting haven for a sensory break. Aedes de Venustas (Temple of Beauty) can make you a signature scent or you can pick from 35 imports from around the world. Lots of celebs pop in here to get their own unique perfume.
☎ 212-206-8674
🖳 www.aedes.com ✉ 9 Christopher St 🕙 noon-8pm Mon-Sat, 1-7pm Sun 🚇 A, B, C, D, E, F, V to W 4th St

Daffy's (3, D6) You'll need to dig at this big, often chaotic discount shop, but you'll be rewarded for your work. There are fab bags, inexpensive Italian-made shoes and a whole 'From Italy' section. Century 21 (p53) is better for big labels, but the occasional Nicole Miller will pop up nonetheless.
☎ 212-334-7444
🖳 www.daffys.com ✉ 462 Broadway 🕙 10am-8pm Mon-Thu, 10am-9pm Fri & Sat, noon-7pm Sun 🚇 N, R to Canal St

Hello Sari (3, E6) Gorgeous silk and chiffon shawls as well as sarongs from Pakistan and India are the specialty of this cozy boutique. Don't overlook the embroidered leather slippers and hand-sewn sandals, which are all the rage right now.
☎ 212-274-0791 ✉ 261 Broome St near Allen St 🕙 11am-7pm Mon-Fri, noon-7pm Sat & Sun; noon-7pm Mon-Fri in winter 🚇 F to Delancey St, F, V to Grand St

It's Another Hit (3, C1) This popular sports memorabilia store is just steps away from Madison Sq Garden and it's a boon for collectors and sports fans alike. It frequently gets hold of high-ticket items, and has a permanent stock of action figures, sports cards and old and new comics.
☎ 212-564-4111
🖳 www.itsanotherhit.com ✉ 131 W 33rd St 🕙 9am-7pm Mon-Fri, 10am-6pm Sat, 11am-6pm Sun 🚇 any train to 34th St/Penn Station

Kate's Paperie (3, D5)
A terrific stationery store that has beautiful hand bound journals, stylish wedding announcements and beautiful paper of all hues. Various locations in the city, including Midtown.
☎ 212-941-9816
🖳 www.katespaperie .com ✉ 561 Broadway 🕙 10am-8pm Mon-Sat, 11am-7pm Sun 🚇 N, R to Prince St

The Rug Company (3, C5)
The Rug Company specializes in contemporary handmade rugs. Most are made from Tibetan wool, which can be customized by size and color. Their designer-rug series features the multicolor Swirl rug by Paul Smith.
☎ 212-274-0444
🖳 www.therugcompany .info ✉ 88 Wooster St 🕙 10am-6pm Mon-Sun 🚇 1, 9, N, R, 6 to Canal St

Shops at Columbus Circle (2, B7) For a mall-like experience in the heart of Manhattan, visit the shops at Columbus Circle. Housed at the base of the Time Warner Center, the more than 50 shops are largely upscale, including Coach, Williams-Sonoma, Hugo Boss, Thomas Pink, Sephora, J Crew, Borders Books & Music, Armani Exchange and Inside CNN.
☎ 212-823-6300
🖳 www.shopsatco lumbuscircle.com ✉ 10 Columbus Circle 🕙 hrs vary depending on shops 🚇 1, 9, A, C, B, D to 59th St-Columbus Circle

Where To Go Next?
- **The Crystal District** Madison Ave from 58th to 63rd Sts is home to Baccarat, Daum, Lalique, Steuben and Swarovski.
- **The Gold Coast** Designer labels only from 59th to 96th Sts (between Fifth Ave and the East River).
- **The Diamond District** Stones are cut, set and sold all along 47th St between Fifth and Sixth Aves.
- **Fashion Row** A tongue-in-cheek name for a string of bargain fashion stores between 18th and 23rd Sts on Sixth Ave.

Eating

Forget everything you thought you knew about cuisine – haute or otherwise – and prepare to be taken to dizzying new culinary heights. It's not uncommon for busy New Yorkers to grab breakfast on the run (bagels, muffins, strong coffee and creamy fruit smoothies are available at just about every corner deli), step out for a quick lunch around noon, and then a communal after-work drink (which often turns into a mid-evening dinner). When time and money permit, nothing is more pleasurable than a hearty brunch – a long, lingering mid-morning affair that involves multiple cups of java, a newspaper shared between friends, and endless plates of eggs, bacon, pancakes, waffles and sandwiches accompanied by crisp salads and flavorful fries. Thanks to the almost continuous parade of new restaurants opening up – each one vying to create the next big fusion trend or reinvent an old standard – your options really are limitless. Even the humble hot dog is given star treatment in this foodie city.

The constant influx of world-class chefs results in plenty of first-rate cooking for those who lust after a truly inimitable dining experience. Classic diners, brasseries, and intimate bistros stud the entire city, and original restaurants with ties to foreign lands are practically ubiquitous. It's not a question of whether you want Chinese tonight, but do you want Szechuan or Mandarin? French Thai or traditional? Big, bean-filled burritos from Northern Mexico or spicy, sauce-laden concoctions with mole and chilis from the Oaxaca region? Every budget and preference can be accommodated in New York City, so eat, drink, and be merry!

> **How Much?**
> The price guide is based on the average cost of a main course with one appetizer. It doesn't include drinks, dessert or tax.
>
> | | |
> |---|---|
> | $ | $12 or less |
> | $$ | $13–22 |
> | $$$ | $23–35 |
> | $$$$ | $36 and above |
>
> Many restaurants, particularly in Lower Manhattan, offer prix fixe meals, which generally average around $20 and include an appetizer, a main, a drink and dessert.

Hot Neighborhoods

There are blocks in this city that catch someone's fancy and before you know it, one, two, three and more restaurants have opened up next to each other. The latest 'Restaurant Row' cropped up in the East Village, along First Ave and 1st St. That in turn led to a mini-restaurant row on Rivington, Orchard and Stanton Sts. Nearby Nolita is still a hot district, with brasseries popping up like mushrooms, while the Upper West Side may be the next trendy locale for grub, thanks to Ouest (p78). But despite all the change, one thing is certain: there will always be restaurants in New York that combine popularity and longevity without sacrificing quality of service or food. And those are the ones you'll find listed here.

LOWER MANHATTAN

Bayard's (3, D8) $$$$
Continental
Formerly the New York Cotton Exchange and now an upscale restaurant with a nautical theme, Bayard's has brought in Eberhard Müller to put this restaurant on the downtown map. Luxurious surroundings demand luxurious dishes and Müller delivers, with inventive sides and sauces to go with mains like roast squab, Dover sole and oven roasted sea bass.
☎ 212-514-9454
🖥 www.bayards.com
✉ 1 Hanover Sq 🕒 dinner Mon-Sat 🚇 2, 3 to Wall St, 4, 5 to Bowling Green

Journey to Bridge Cafe for the views and the vibe

Bridge Cafe (3, D7) $$
American creative
Opened in 1794, this worn-in tavern under the Brooklyn Bridge offers an extensive wine list and dressed-up standard American fare including pastas, seafood, roasted meats and luscious chocolate desserts. Its old-world flavor imbues everything with a very romantic vibe.
☎ 212-227-3344 ✉ 279 Water St at Dover St 🕒 lunch, dinner Mon-Fri, dinner Sat 🚇 2, 3, 4, 5, A, C, J, M, Z to Fulton St-Broadway Nassau ♿ fair 🍴 for lunch

Cuban (3, D8) $
Cuban
Steaming hot plates of rice and beans topped with onion and cilantro really hit the spot, as do the crispy tostones and the dark caffè con leche. Lots of downtown workers cram in for a quick bite before heading back to work but by 2pm there's usually plenty of room.
☎ 212-269-0909
✉ Pearl St btwn Maiden Lane & Platt St 🕒 lunch Mon-Fri 🚇 2, 3 to Wall St 🍴

F.illi Ponte (3, B6) $$$$
Italian
The downstairs bar replete with Italian sparkling wine, reds and whites from around the world (including some Long Island vineyards) is reason enough to come, but don't miss the gorgeous beamed ceilings and creamy Italian dishes in the restaurant upstairs.
☎ 212-226-4621
🖥 www.filliponte.com
✉ 39 Desbrosses St 🕒 dinner Mon, lunch & dinner Tue-Fri & Sat 🚇 1, 2, 3, 9 to Chambers St 🍴 🅥

Les Halles (3, D8) $$$
French
Somewhat hidden on dingy John St, Les Halles' dark front doors open into a bustling and fragrant atmosphere, filled with discreetly dressed patrons dining on warm potato salad, escargots and other classic French fare. Those with less appetite can choose a roast chicken sandwich or some gourmet mac-and-cheese.
☎ 212-285-8585
🖥 www.leshalles.net
✉ 15 John St btwn Broadway & Nassau St 🕒 lunch, dinner 🚇 A, C to Broadway-Nassau St

Paris Bar & Grill (3, D8) $$
American creative
The Paris started serving customers in 1873 and really never stopped, although ownership changed several times. It's got the most beautiful curving bar in town and plenty of fresh seafood right from Fulton St Fishmarket. Chicken dishes, steaks and hearty desserts round out the menu, and the prix fixe lunch at $19.95 is a good deal. Now Irish-run, it's open late for drinking.
☎ 212-240-9797
🖥 www.theparistavern .com ✉ 119 South St at Peck Slip 🕒 11am-2am 🚇 2, 3 to Wall St ♿ fair 🍴 for lunch

SOHO/TRIBECA

Bubby's (3, C6) $$
Comfort food
Famous for its mac-and-cheese, Bubby's does upscale comfort food like slow-cooked BBQ, grits and juicy ribs. Innovative brunch dishes like the Eggsadilla (similar to a quesadilla but done with eggs) and salmon florentine are great any time of day.
☎ 212-219-0666
🖥 www.bubbys.com
✉ 120 Hudson St at N Moore St ✆ breakfast, lunch & dinner, brunch Sun Ⓒ 1, 9 to Franklin St ♿

Blue Ribbon (3, C5) $$$
Comfort food
Not quite the usual comfort food, but enticing nonetheless. Bruce and Eric Bromberg – chefs, owners and brothers – offer the city's best raw bar, as well as oxtail marmalade, seafood paella, a tofu-seaweed salad so juicy you'll need two napkins and crispy fried chicken.
☎ 212-274-0404
🖥 www.blueribbon restaurants.com ✉ 97 Sullivan St ✆ dinner, open until 4am Ⓒ C, E to Spring St, N, R to Prince St

Capsouto Frères (3, B6) $$–$$$
French
Lovely atmosphere and impeccable service are the hallmarks of this gorgeous bistro, owned by a trio of brothers with a fascinating family history. Most famous for soufflés, the restaurant also has wonderful chef specials like stuffed zucchini blossoms with goat's cheese and loin of lamb. Very romantic settings, but children are welcome – the kitchen can make small portions of some dishes.
☎ 212-966-4900
🖥 www.capsoutofreres .com ✉ 451 Washington St at Watts St ✆ dinner Mon, lunch & dinner Tue-Fri, brunch & dinner Sat & Sun Ⓒ 1, 9 to Canal St ♿

Franklin St Station (3, C6) $
Southeast Asian/French
An endearingly offbeat restaurant, Franklin St has great Asian beers, a lovely wine list and food ranging between Asian and French. There are delicious Malaysian curry dishes, lots of artfully presented salads, thick mango smoothies and hearty soups. Keep an eye on the slideshow that's sometimes projected on the wall – gorgeous images to go with impeccable food.
☎ 212-274-8525 ✉ 222 W Broadway at Franklin St ✆ breakfast, lunch & dinner daily, brunch Sat & Sun Ⓒ 1, 9 to Franklin St, A, C, E to Canal St ♿

L'Orange Bleue (3, D6) $$
African/Moroccan French
A cheery room full of softly lit Moroccan lamps that make the warm orange walls glow, this restaurant has an earthy, friendly vibe that keeps everybody coming back. The menu is inventive without being too exotic; amid the tagines and yellowfin tuna with mango salsa are staples like garlic mashed potatoes and yummy salads.
☎ 212-226-4999
🖥 www.lorangebleue.tv
✉ 430 Broome St at Crosby St ✆ dinner Mon-Fri, brunch & dinner Sat & Sun Ⓒ 6 to Spring St, N, R to Prince St

Nolita Charmers

- **Café Colonial** (3, D5; Houston & Elizabeth Sts; $–$$) Creative Brazilian in cozy settings
- **Café Lebowitz** (3, D5; 14 Spring St; $–$$) Parisian ambience for the literati
- **Lovely Day** (3, D5; 196 Elizabeth St; $–$$) Chic and casual with cute red booths
- **Mekong** (3, D5; 44 Prince St; $–$$) Heady Vietnamese dishes of all sorts and outdoor tables
- **Porcupine** (3, D5; 20 Prince St; $–$$) Divine steak frites and warm service
- **Public** (3, D5; 210 Elizabeth St; $$$) Beloved for its faux-library decor and big menu
- **Xicala** (3, D6; 151 Elizabeth St; $–$$) Brooding but endearing, with great tapas and wine

CHINATOWN & LITTLE ITALY

Da Gennaro (3, D6) $$
Italian
A cut above many of the tourist traps that can be found along Mulberry St, Da Gennaro has spicy pasta sauces, classic Italian parmigiana dishes and lots of chicken, steak and seafood on the menu, as well as delicious meatball sandwiches.
☎ 212-431-3934 ✉ 129 Mulberry St ⏱ lunch, dinner Ⓔ J, M, N, Q, R, W, Z, 6 to Canal St ♿

Mexican Radio (3, D6) $$
Mexican
Lots of soft lighting and warm red walls with kitschy decor make Mexican Radio a very relaxing, comforting place to hang out. The burritos are big and authentic, as are the flautas, fajitas and carnitas. If you've still got room after one of these big meals, go next door to Eileen's for some magnificent cheesecake. You won't regret it.
☎ 212-343-0140 🖥 www.mexrad.com ✉ 19 Cleveland Pl ⏱ lunch, dinner Ⓔ 6 to Spring St ♿ fair ♿ great atmosphere for kids Ⓥ

Nha Trang (3, D6) $
Vietnamese
Big, bustling Nha Trang is very popular with workers in the surrounding downtown courts, and is especially famous for its *pho*, the beef-and-rice-noodle soup that's a staple for Vietnamese. Other dishes to try include chicken

Lombardi's (p72): traditional pizza from a traditional oven

with lemongrass or spicy veggies with beancurd.
☎ 212-233-5948 ✉ 87 Baxter St at Bayard St ⏱ lunch, dinner Ⓔ J, M, N, Q, R, W, Z, 6 to Canal St ♿ fair ♿ Ⓥ

Rice (3, D5) $
Asian fusion
Nature's most prolific grain is on the menu here, and once you've had a mouthful of the moist green rice (infused with cilantro, parsley and spinach) or the Thai black rice (sticky, tender and steamed in coconut milk) you'll be hooked. The shrimp satay with a warm sauce of roasted almonds is succulent, as is the tea-smoked salmon salad on mixed greens with ginger hoisin vinaigrette.
☎ 212-226-5775 🖥 www.riceny.com ✉ 227 Mott St ⏱ noon-midnight Ⓔ 6 to Spring St ♿ fair ♿ Ⓥ

Ruby's (3, D5) $
Eclectic
A little eatery on busy Mulberry St, Ruby's has whole grain sandwiches and lovely fresh salads. But

the best deal on the menu is the all-day breakfast featuring toasted Turkish bread, organic oatmeal, egg sandwiches, deep, dark coffees and banana mango smoothies — something for everyone!
☎ 212-925-5755 ✉ 219 Mulberry St ⏱ 11am-11pm Mon-Fri, 4-11pm Sat & Sun Ⓔ 6 to Spring St ♿ fair ♿

X O Café (3, D6) $
Chinese
You know a place is good when it's full of locals, and that's the case here. On the downside, the waiters get so busy that sometimes service can be a tad slow. But once they get moving everything comes fast — the dishes are authentic, well-prepared and seasoned just right. The salt-baked shrimp is a knockout, as are the shrimp lo mein, and chicken over black bean sauce.
☎ 212-343-8625 ✉ 96 Walker St at Lafayette St ⏱ 10am-11pm Mon-Sat, 10am-9pm Sun Ⓔ J, M, N, Q, R, W, Z, 6 to Canal St ♿ fair ♿ Ⓥ

EAST VILLAGE

Boca Chica (3, D5) $–$$
Pan-Latin American
Serving fresh, innovative food from all over Latin America, with the occasional hint of Asian fusion, Boca Chica is always packed (no reservations accepted). It's delicious and fun; *arroz con pollo* (chicken and rice) and *ropa vieja* (shredded beef) are at their succulent, steaming best.
☎ 212-473-0108
✉ 13 First Ave, at E 1st St
🕒 brunch Sun, dinner
🚇 F to Second Ave
♿ good ⏱

Brick Lane Curry House (3, D4) $$
Indian
There's lots of Indian fare along Sixth Ave, but this pretty little place stands out for two reasons: the decor is bright and attractive, and the food is sublime. The chicken tikka masala and lamb vindaloo are among the best in the city.
☎ 212-979-8787
🖥 bricklanecurryhouse .com ✉ 306-308 E 6th St
🕒 lunch, dinner 🚇 6 to Astor Pl ♿ fair ⏱ Ⓥ

Chez Es Saada (3, D5) $$$
Moroccan/Southern soul
Its sexy, swanky bar has always been a hot spot for a cool drink, but now the food is earning raves too. The latest menu has a lot of spicy North African influences mixed with Middle Eastern fare.
☎ 212-777-5617
🖥 www.chezessaada .com ✉ 42 E 1st St
🕒 dinner Mon-Sat

🚇 F, V to Second Ave-Lower East Side

Dawgs on Park (3, E4) $
Hot dogs
The all-beef dogs are deep-fried, but the homemade bean chili is vegan. Grab a stool and look out at Tompkins Sq Park while you chomp your dog (turkey and tofu choices available) dripping with corn salsa, ketchup, or the classic mustard and kraut.
☎ 212-598-0667
🖥 www.dawgsonpark .com ✉ 178 E 7th St btwn Aves A & B
🕒 lunch, dinner 🚇 F, V to Lower East Side-Second Ave ♿ fair ⏱ Ⓥ

Katz's Deli (3, E5) $
Jewish deli
The smell of cured deli meats and a sense of urgency are hallmarks of Katz's Deli, a beloved New York eatery that serves sandwiches the size of your arm. Lines move lightning fast and you have to be ready to order at a moment's notice – grab a table if you want slower service.
☎ 212-254-2246
🖥 www.katzdeli.com
✉ 205 E Houston St at Ludlow St 🕒 breakfast, lunch, dinner 🚇 F, V to Lower East Side-Second Ave ♿ fair ⏱ Ⓥ

Prune (3, D5) $$
American
With its eclectic, but familiar menu, Prune is a delight. Staple veggies like creamed corn are matched by big meat mains such as capon on a savory garlic crouton, or pastrami duck breast with a fried-shallot omelet. Brunch is popular, with heart-stopping Monte Cristos, honey-flavored oatmeal, perfectly cooked eggs, and nine (count 'em) variations on a Bloody Mary.
☎ 212-677-6221
🖥 www.prunerestaur ant.com ✉ 54 E 1st St
🕒 brunch Sat & Sun, dinner 🚇 F, V to Lower East Side-Second Ave

Renaissance on the Loisada

Some of the hottest restaurants are amidst the dilapidated tenements of the Lower East Side, which add to rather than detract from the experience.

- **Schillers Liquor Bar** (3, E5; 131 Rivington St; $$) Fantastic, flavorful food – Welsh rarebit, steak frites, garlic shrimp, toffee pudding – and unpretentious service make this place glow.
- **WD-50** (3, E5; 50 Clinton St; $$$) Artistically piled food – the calamari castle has a lemon wedge moat – feeds the eye as well as the mouth.
- **'Inoteca** (3, E5; 98 Rivington St; $$) Wine flows freely (200 bottles in-house) amidst plates of paninis, eggplant and other Italian snacks.

WEST VILLAGE

Annisa (3, C4) $$$
American/French
Chef and co-owner Anita Lo has created a multicultural feast at Annisa. Oysters with three root vegetables, grilled fillet of redfish with chorizo bread salad and spicy grilled eggplant with lentils speak to her range. Trading on the restaurant's name (which means 'women' in Arabic), Lo's impressive wine list comes almost exclusively from female vintners or female-run vineyards.
☎ 212-741-6699
🖳 www.annisarestaur
ant.com ✉ 13 Barrow St
🕑 dinner Mon-Sat ◎ 1, 9 to Christopher St, A, C, E, B, D, F, V to W 4th St
♿ fair Ⓥ

Babbo (3, C4) $$$$
Italian
The magic of chef Mario Batali is apparent after the first bite of fennel-dusted sweetbreads with duck bacon and vinegar. Combining rarely used ingredients, he turns out savory creations that dance on the palate and glow in the belly.
☎ 212-777-0303
🖳 http://babbonyc.com

✉ 110 Waverly Pl
🕑 dinner ◎ A, C, E, B, D, F, V to W 4th St, 1, 9 to Christopher St

Gotham Bar & Grill (3, C4) $$$$
American
For 20 years this restaurant has been held in high regard by the public and the critics. Its luxurious setting and discreet service count for a lot, but it's the delicate risottos, rich terrines and savory grilled fishes that really please the masses.
☎ 212-620-4020
🖳 http://gothambarand
grill.com ✉ 12 E 12th St btwn University Pl & Fifth Ave 🕑 lunch Mon-Fri, dinner ◎ 4, 5, 6, L, N, Q, R, W to Union Sq

Home (3, C4) $$
American
As fresh and cozy as it was when it opened in 1994, Home still features Midwestern-style cooking with a few innovations, like roasted chicken, garlicky greens and spicy onion rings. Brunches on weekends are extremely popular.
☎ 212-243-9579

🖳 www.recipesfrom
home.com ✉ 20 Cornelia St btwn Bleecker & W 4th Sts 🕑 breakfast, lunch & dinner Mon-Fri, brunch & dinner Sat & Sun ◎ A, B, C, D, E, F, V to W 4th St
♿ except dinner

Petite Abeille (3, B5) $$
Belgian
There's barely room for more than three customers at a time at this West Village eatery, but the Belgian waffles, double-dipped fries and prix-fixe menu ($20 including a beer) more than make up for the cramped quarters. For those who want to spread out, there's a larger location in the Meatpacking District.
☎ 212-741-6479
🖳 www.petiteabeille
.com ✉ 466 Hudson St
🕑 lunch, dinner ◎ 1, 9 to Christopher St-Sheridan Sq ♿ fair ⚡ Ⓥ

Surya (3, B4) $$
Nouvelle Indian
A fabulous dining experience, Surya's sleek and elegant decor mingles wonderfully with the food, friendly atmosphere and impressive wine list (there are also luscious cocktails; try the one with rose petals). Vegetarians will love the vegetable korma and all-veggie appetizers; for meat eaters, the chicken pakora, grilled fish dishes and spicy lamb vindaloos always win raves.
☎ 212-807-7770
🖳 www.suryany.com
✉ 302 Bleecker St
🕑 dinner Mon-Sat ◎ 1, 9 to Christopher St-Sheridan Sq ♿ fair Ⓥ

Brown is the new black, but Gotham is always in fashion

MEATPACKING DISTRICT/CHELSEA

Amuse (3, C3) $$
American
You'll love grazing on the small plates of Amuse Fries (made with chipotle and aioli), olive poached tuna, braised beets or roasted shiitake mushrooms (to name but a few). To try it all get the prix-fixe sampler.
☎ 212-929-9755
🖥 www.amusenyc.com
✉ 108 W 18th St
🕐 lunch & dinner Mon-Fri, dinner Sat ⊖ F, V to 14th St ♿

Empire Diner (3, A3) $-$$
Diner
A throwback to the days when much of the far West Side of Manhattan was involved in risky business, the Empire Diner has an old-school (read eccentric) kind of charm. Housed in a silver Pullman car, the Empire has granite-thick chocolate shakes, burgers with lentils on top and fat omelets stuffed with whatever you want.
☎ 212-243-2736
🖥 www.theempirediner.com ✉ 210 Tenth Ave at 22nd St 🕐 24hr ⊖ C, E to 23rd St ♿ fair ♿ Ⓥ

Florent (3, B4) $-$$
French/Diner
Everybody who's anybody passes through this unpretentious joint at one time or another. A fixture on the West Side, Florent has huge juicy burgers, great lentil salad, mussels, blood sausage and rich, decadent desserts. The crowds come and go in waves: the after-theater group, the late-

The last of the big spenders at Florent

night clubbing group, then the really, really late-night clubbing group.
☎ 212-989-5779
🖥 www.restaurant florent.com ✉ 69 Gansevoort St 🕐 breakfast, lunch, dinner Mon-Thu, 24hr Fri-Sun ⊖ A, C, E to 14th St ♿ fair ♿ Ⓥ

Macelleria (3, B4) $$
Italian
Rough wooden tables, low ceilings and an imposing oak bar go well with Macelleria's no-holds-barred approach to serving up large, appetizing cuts of meat. The name means 'butcher shop' in Italian and the menu is unapologetically carnivorous, with a few pasta dishes and soups to round things out.
☎ 212-741-2555
🖥 macelleria@aol.com
✉ 48 Gansevoort St
🕐 lunch & dinner Mon-Fri, brunch & dinner Sat & Sun ⊖ A, C, E, L to 14th St ♿ fair

Pastis (3, B4) $-$$
French
Pastis is a working-class bistro for the ages. The shining railings, beautiful tiles, hustle

bustle and constant chatter are denigrated by some who find it noisy, but it's a popular place, a locus of neighborhood life. Follow your heart and belly up for steak frites, croque monsieur, leg of lamb or braised beef. You won't be disappointed.
☎ 212-929-4844
🖥 www.pastisny.com
✉ Ninth Ave at Little W 12th St 🕐 breakfast, lunch & dinner Mon-Fri, brunch & dinner Sat & Sun ⊖ 1,9, 2, 3, A, C, E, L to 14th St ♿ fair ♿

The Red Cat (3, A2) $-$$
Mediterranean/American
Tucked between Chelsea galleries and frequented by not-so-starving artists, The Red Cat sports local art, barn doors and swinging lantern lights. Stand out dishes include roasted cod with sweet pea risotto, parmesan french fries and roast chicken with a salad of garden vegetables. Lots of celebs appear here; reservations suggested.
☎ 212-242-1122
🖥 www.theredcat.com
✉ 227 Tenth Ave btwn 23rd & 24th Sts 🕐 dinner ⊖ 1, 9, C, E to 23rd St

UNION SQUARE/FLATIRON DISTRICT/GRAMERCY PARK

Craft (3, C3) $$$
American
The menu comes with more subdivisions than the Lower East Side – food is divided by type (veggie, fish, poultry, meat) and cooking method (raw, braised, grilled etc). It works because everything is super fresh, and famously picky New Yorkers don't mind designing meals from top to bottom. Try any of the fresh salmon, sea bass or halibut grills for a real treat.
☎ 212-780-0880
🖳 www.craftrestaurant.com ✉ 43 E 19th St ⏱ lunch Mon-Fri, dinner ⊕ 4, 5, 6, L, N, Q, R, W to 14th St Ⓥ

Craftbar (3, C3) $–$$
American/Italian
A scaled-down version of the foodie-frenzy at Craft, this sibling location uses the same ultra-fresh ingredients but puts them in already assembled meals. Sizzling paninis, deep-dish risottos, braised fish dishes and vegetable-laden pastas are house specialties.
☎ 212-780-0880 ✉ 47 East 19th St ⏱ lunch, dinner ⊕ 4, 5, 6, L, N, Q, R, W to 14th St Ⓐ lunch Ⓥ

Eisenberg's Sandwich Shop (3, C3) $
American diner
When you need an oversize sandwich that won't put a serious dent in your pocket, step inside this time capsule and get whisked back to 1929, the year Eisenberg's opened. Kids love the super-narrow vintage bar and adults appreciate the good turkey clubs, reubens, and bacon-and-egg sandwiches served here.
☎ 212-675-5096 ✉ 174 Fifth Ave ⏱ lunch ⊕ 6, N, R to 23rd St Ⓐ ideal for children

Eleven Madison Park (3, C2) $$$$
French
Located inside the Met Life Building, Eleven Madison Park has a surfeit of space that gives diners a lot of breathing room, a rarity in crowded New York. Children do well here and the service is very flexible and friendly. Stick to the big simple dishes like roasted free-range chicken with mashed potatoes, grilled steak with creamed spinach or cod with sausage. The bar is a popular hang out for well-heeled thirty-somethings.
☎ 212-889-0905 🖳 www.elevenmadisonpark.com ✉ 11 Madison Ave ⏱ lunch,

---

La Crème de la Crème

A list of some of the best deals in town, with options in all price ranges.

- Best sandwich: **Vietnam Bánh mì So # 1** (3, D6; ☎ 212-219-8341; 369 Broome St near Mott St; $) Fancy a Vietnamese style meatball sub? Banh Mi So #1 makes 11 types of delectable sandwiches.
- Best brunch: **Norma's** (2, C7; ☎ 212-708-7460; 118 W 57th St at Sixth Ave; $$-$$$) The most luxurious, decadent breakfast in town, served on the ground floor of the Parker Meridien Hotel.
- Best pizza: **Lombardi's** (3, D5; ☎ 212-941-7994; 32 Spring St; $-$$) Thin or thick crust, clams, veggies, or just cheese on top – no matter how you slice it, this pizza is the best.
- Best Malaysian: **Nyonya** (3, D6; ☎ 212-334-3669; 194 Grand St btwn Mott & Mulberry Sts; $) A legend among ex-pat Malaysians, Nyonya has great seafood delights.
- Best steak au poivre with soothsayer: **Seppi's** (2, C7; ☎ 212-708-7444; 123 W 56th St; $$-$$$) Seppi's warm and elegant ambiance is a perfect foil for chef-owner Claude Solliard's whimsical and inventive culinary creations. The occasional torch singer drops in to perform and there's a tarot card reader stationed near the front door. Bon appetit!

dinner 🕐 6, N, R to 23rd St ⚿ good ⚿

Gramercy Tavern (3, C3) $$$

American

It will take some planning to get a table at this restaurant, but by all means go for it. Celebrity chef Tom Colicchio (of Craft and Craftbar as well) works his magic here with braised beef cheeks and crabmeat fondue, not to mention braised rabbit over shallots and portobello-mushroom tarts. And the sinfully delicious desserts? Made in-house, of course.
☎ 212-477-0777
🖥 http://gramercytavern.com ✉ 42 E 20th St
🕐 lunch Mon-Fri, dinner
🕐 6, N, R, W to 23rd St

Madras Mahal (3, D2) $–$$

Indian

A vegetarian and kosher delight, Madras Mahal makes paper-thin *dosas* (rice crepes) and then wraps them around savory mixtures of masala potatoes, peas, cilantro and other spicy herbs. More traditional dishes like *saag panir* (spinach with spices)

Veggie Deluxe

- **Angelica's Kitchen** (3, D4; 300 E 12th St; $–$$) Creative, cleansing vegan fare for everyone
- **Bonobos** (3, C3; 18 E 23rd St; $) Take-out salads and make-your-own plates of 'live' raw ingredients
- **Pure Food & Wine** (3, D3; 54 Irving Pl btwn 17th & 18th Sts; $$) White-hot with raw foodists; the best kitchen in town – minus the stove
- **Vegetarian Dim Sum House** (3, D6; 24 Pell St; $) Alarmingly meat-like BBQ 'ribs' and yummy squash soups

and fried samosas are also served to great acclaim.
☎ 212-684-4010
🖥 www.madrasmahal.com ✉ 104 Lexington Ave 🕐 lunch, dinner
🕐 6 to 28th St Ⓥ

Patria (3, D3) $$$

Latin American

Three light-filled floors full of airy, colorful decor have turned Patria into a perennial favorite among the dining out crowd. The Cuban sandwiches are fantastic, as are the surprisingly non-greasy empanadas and garlic-infused seafood dishes.
☎ 212-777-6211 ✉ 250 Park Ave Sth 🕐 lunch Mon-Fri, dinner 🕐 6, N, R to 23rd St ⚿ fair

Tabla (3, C2) $$$

Indian

It's hard to know how chef Floyd Cardoz manages to combine American staples like pork and crab with delicate seasonings and sauces from his native Delhi, but he does it – again and again. Try the Goan-spiced Maine lobster, green beans in coconut curry or the mushroom kabob with braised fennel, all served with fruity, flowery flourishes. For a more casual experience head to **Bread Bar** on the ground floor for straight-up Indian food.
☎ 212-889-0667 ✉ 11 Madison Ave 🕐 lunch Mon-Fri, dinner 🕐 6, N, R to 23rd St Ⓥ

Design your own meal with other invisible diners at Craft restaurant

FOR THE FAMILY

America (3, C3) $$
American
Weekend brunches have balloon artists and clowns, kids can get as much mac-and-cheese as they like, and for adults there's spicy Buffalo wings, blue cheese salads and a weekday happy hour.
☎ 212-505-2110 ✉ 9 E 18th St ⏰ breakfast & dinner Mon-Fri, brunch & dinner Sat & Sun ⊕ 6, N, R to 23rd St ♿

Cafe Un Deux Trois (2, C8) $$
French bistro
Cups of crayons and paper placemats are freely doled out by welcoming staff, who also serve size-appropriate portions of warm comfort food. The menu has family-friendly dishes like spaghetti and meatballs, chicken noodle soup and french fries.
☎ 212-354-4148 🖳 cafe undeuxtrois.biz ✉ 123 W 44th St ⏰ noon-11pm ⊕ any to Times Sq ♿

Fresh (3, C7) $$$
Seafood
Kids who love seafood will be entranced with Fresh, where minimalist surroundings are off-set by smiling staff who happily hand out lobster bibs. Fresh shrimp, clams and mussels can be fried, baked or breaded, and desserts like tapioca pudding add a homey touch.
☎ 212-406-1900 🖳 http://freshrestaur ant.com ✉ 105 Reade St ⏰ dinner Mon-Sat ⊕ 1, 2, 3, 9, A, C, E to Chambers St ♿

Lexington's finest candy shop – for kids *and* grown-ups

Grilled Cheese NYC (3, E5) $
Grilled cheese
Every combination of grilled cheese you could imagine (and more) is available at this late-night and family-friendly spot. Some of the more complicated variations feature meat and veggie inserts, but whether your child likes his or her sandwich classic or experimental, the chef will make it to order.
☎ 212-982-6600 🖳 http://grilledcheese nyc.com ✉ 168 Ludlow St ⏰ lunch, dinner ⊕ F, V to Second Ave ♿

Lexington Candy Shop (2, D4) $
American
Lots of toys and playthings are scattered about in this narrow, 1930s-style diner. Kids are welcome to jump up on the stools and spin themselves around or color with crayons in the booths. Milkshakes, good fries, and the usual hamburgers and sandwiches are on offer.
☎ 212-288-0057 ✉ 1226 Lexington Ave ⏰ 9am-9pm Mon-Sat, 10am-6pm Sun ⊕ 4, 5, 6 to 77th St ♿

Osteria del Circo (2, C7) $$$
Italian
If your kids are ready for some upscale dining, this is the place to start. The chef is happy to make simplified dishes for them while giving you the full treatment, especially if you come early. Order up some Shirley Temples and individual pizzas and let the fun begin!
☎ 212-265-3636 🖳 www.osteriadelcirco .com ✉ 120 W 55th St ⏰ lunch Mon-Fri, dinner ⊕ N, R to 57th St ♿

Peanut Butter & Co (3, C5) $
American/Vegetarian
Did you think creamy and chunky were your only options? You've got 21 ways to eat your peanut butter and for the indecisive child, this can be traumatic. Choices include peanut butter on celery sticks and studded with raisins, or the 'Elvis,' a grilled peanut butter, bacon, honey and banana sandwich on whole wheat.
☎ 212-677-3995 🖳 www.ilovepeanutbut ter.com ✉ 240 Sullivan St ⏰ lunch, dinner ⊕ A, C, E, F, V to W 4th St ♿

MIDTOWN

44 & X – Hell's Kitchen (2, B8)
$$–$$$
Comfort/American
Way over yonder on Tenth Ave a buzzing, light-filled restaurant has opened up to great acclaim. The food is a combination of comfort (turkey and gravy) and innovative (lobster-stuffed tacos with chipotle salsa). It's exciting, different, and just a little bit daring – kind of like the street it's on.
☎ 212-977-1170
🖥 www.44andx.com
✉ 622 Tenth Ave at 44th St ☽ dinner ⊕ any train to 42nd St-Times Sq/Port Authority

Cho Dang Goi (2, C9) $–$$
Korean
Right in the heart of Koreatown, Cho Dang Goi does a brisk business in traditional *bibimbops* (vegetables with rice and spicy sauce), sticky-rice dishes and pork stews, which are all among the best in the area. You'll also get the tiny plates of kimchi surprises (including a pile of teensy dried fish, eyes intact) right before your meal begins.
☎ 212-695-8222 ✉ 55 W 35th St ☽ lunch, dinner ⊕ B, D, F, V, N, Q, R, W to 34th St/Herald Sq ☂

DB Bistro Moderne (2, C8)
$$$$
French
When you start hankering for a hamburger stuffed with truffle, and foie gras–laced short ribs, accompanied by pommes soufflées, then you visit DB Bistro Moderne. Chef extraordinaire Daniel Boulud's menu is laden down with classic country (French) cooking: stuffed pigs' feet, cassoulet, and foie gras and apricot tartlet, to name only a few. As always, Boulud's food is good to the last bite.
☎ 212-391-2400
🖥 http://danielnyc.com
✉ 55 W 44th St ☽ lunch & dinner Mon-Sat (no Sat lunch in summer), dinner Sun ⊕ 7, B, D, F, V to 42nd St/Bryant Park

Esca (2, B8)
$$$
Italian
It's all about seafood at Mario Batali's latest gold star restaurant: there's an incredible raw bar of the highest quality, a one-pound lobster, and a whole fish for two. Then there's the wine list, an admirable compilation of vintages that go perfectly with the food.
☎ 212-564-7272 🖥 www .esca-nyc.com ✉ 402 W 43rd St ☽ lunch, dinner Mon-Sat, dinner Sun ⊕ A, C, E to 42nd St

Island Burgers & Shakes (2, B7)
$
American/Mexican
Try any of the burgers and chicken sandwiches, or blackened and grilled fish dishes that come with your choice of sides, as well as fresh sandwiches offered in numerous combinations on chewy semolina bread.
☎ 212-307-7934 ✉ 766 Ninth Ave ☽ lunch, dinner ⊕ C, E to 50th St

Le Bateau Ivre (2, E7) $$
French
With more than 150 varieties of wine available by the glass, this restaurant has earned its name ('the drunken boat'). The French bistro fare with Belgian touches (moules marinières, pommes frites) is good without being fussy, but the wine list and relaxed atmosphere are the most impressive things about this charming spot.
☎ 212-583-0579 ✉ 230 E 51st St ☽ breakfast, lunch & dinner ⊕ 6 to 51st/Lexington Ave ☂ fair ☃

Le Bernardin (2, C7) $$$$
French seafood
Nowhere else in town will you get a full sensory dining experience like the one offered at Le Bernardin. Typical

An island of burgers and shakes in the gulf of Mexico

Taking Care of Business
New Yorkers love the power lunch (and brunch and dinner) and know just where to go to seal the deal. **Eleven Madison Park** (p72) is perfect for very private meetings. Important job interviews are handled at **Bayard's** (p66). If you're hosting foreign clients **Le Bernadin** (p75) is the spot, and **Gotham Bar & Grill** (p70) works for slightly less-formal gatherings. When you need to go all out, it has to be **Jean-Georges** (p78).

dishes: whole red snapper baked in a rosemary-and-thyme crust, or striped bass with roasted foie gras. The food, the ambience and even the waiters are in harmony. It's a perfect experience.
☎ 212-489-1515
🖳 http://le-bernardin .com ✉ 155 W 51st St
☽ lunch Mon-Fri, dinner Mon-Sat ⊕ B, D, F, Q to 47th/50th Sts

Marichu (2, E8) $$$
Spanish/Tapas
Great for long, lingering lunches, Marichu usually caters to the UN crowd during the day and a comfortable thirty-something crowd in the evening. Serving hearty country food that fuses the best of Spanish and Basque cuisines and rustic red wines, Marichu is a solid winner.
☎ 212-370-1866
🖳 www.marichu.com
✉ 342 E 46th St
☽ lunch & dinner Mon-Fri, dinner Sat & Sun ⊕ S, 4, 5, 6, 7 to 42nd St-Grand Central ♿ fair

Marseille (2, B8) $$
Mediterranean/Southern soul
An unlikely combination of cuisines has created a big buzz around Marseille, a

beautiful eatery in the Film Center Building that dares to offer bouillabaisse alongside deep-fried chicken, and pan-fried white corn next to classic blood sausage.
☎ 212-333-3410
🖳 www.marseillenyc .com ✉ 630 Ninth Ave
☽ lunch & dinner Mon-Fri, brunch & dinner Sat & Sun ⊕ any train to 42nd St-Times Sq/Port Authority ♿ fair

Meskerem (2, B8) $$
Ethiopian
Fiery sauces go well with garlicky chunks of meat and chicken dishes, while vegetarians will be very happy with the many dishes based on chick peas, lentils, carrots and beans. Mop it all up with spongy pieces of *injera,* a flat, sourdough-like bread that is a staple of the Ethiopian diet.
☎ 212-664-0520
🖳 www.meskeremres taurant.com ✉ 468 W 47th St ☽ lunch, dinner ⊕ C, E to 50th St Ⓥ

Turkish Kitchen (3, D2) $$
Turkish/Middle Eastern
Hidden behind a mesmerizing glass entranceway,

Turkish Kitchen has deep red walls, beautiful lighting and fresh-cut flowers at each table. The colors are sexy, the food sensuous, and the Bosphorus Martini is out of this world. Any of the pirzolas (chicken or lamb) are great, as are the fish dishes.
☎ 212-679-6633
🖳 www.turkishkitch enny.com ✉ 386 Third Ave ☽ lunch & dinner Mon-Fri, dinner only Sat & Sun ⊕ 6 to 28th St

Uncle Nick's (2, B7) $$
Greek
A tiny Greek restaurant on Manhattan's West Side, Uncle Nick's is a busy, family-friendly, upbeat locale that everyone seems to love. Some of the dishes don't score high on the American palate – *mezedakia* (calves' livers), for example – but the poultry, grilled fishes, salty garlicky appetizers and warm, fresh bread never fail to please.
☎ 212-245-7992 ✉ 747 Ninth Ave ☽ lunch Sun-Thu, dinner ⊕ C, E to 50th St, 1, 9 to 49th St ♿

Vong (2, D7) $$$
Thai
Gorgeous colors and sumptuous decorations are a hallmark of this Jean-Georges Vongerichten eatery. The passion fruit martinis go down easy, as do the slow-baked salmon with tomato marmalade and other French-Thai fusion mains.
☎ 212-486-9592
🖳 www.jean-georges .com ✉ 200 E 54th St
☽ lunch & dinner Mon-Fri, dinner Sat ⊕ E, F, 6 to 51st St/Lexington Ave Ⓥ

UPPER EAST SIDE

Cafe Sabarsky (2, D4) $$
Austrian
On the 1st floor of the Neue Galerie Museum and across the street from leafy Central Park, this is the perfect place for a Museum Mile break. The beef goulash is steaming hot, the cod strudel and tangy herring sandwich flavored just right, and the rich little cakes go well with a strong coffee.
☎ 212-288-0665
🖳 www.wallse.com
✉ Neue Galerie New York, 1048 Fifth Ave at 86th St
🕑 breakfast, lunch, dinner 🚇 4, 5, 6 to 86th St

Daniel (2, D6) $$$$
French
A spacious, romantic haven with gentle lighting, Daniel's will woo you with plates of peeky toe crab and celery-root salad, followed by cod confit with fennel, grapefruit, chick peas and cardamom, or short ribs braised in red wine with creamy celery 'mousseline.' The sommelier will happily help you select a great wine, and don't miss the chocolate bombe dessert.
☎ 212-288-0033
🖳 http://danielnyc.com
✉ 60 E 65th St 🕑 dinner Mon-Sat 🚇 6 to 68th St

Erminia (2, E4) $$$
Italian
Dark and intimate, with tables lit only by candles, Erminia's has a two-week waiting list and a stellar reputation. Regulars come for the ambience and the food, particularly the linguine with white clam sauce, stuffed veal, wood-fired fish skewers and perfectly seasoned lamb chops.
☎ 212-879-4284 ✉ 250 E 83rd St 🕑 dinner Mon-Sat 🚇 4, 5, 6 to 86th St

Etats-Unis (2, E4) $$$
American
The daily-changing menu choices at Etats-Unis consistently feature great vegetables and choice meats. Juicy grilled steaks, tender lamb kabobs and roast beef can be had, as well as thick creamy soups that stand alone as a meal. The desserts – airy and rich at the same time – end every meal on the right note.
☎ 212-517-8826 ✉ 242 E 81st St 🕑 dinner 🚇 4, 5, 6 to 86th St

Pamir (2, E5) $$
Mediterranean/Middle Eastern
Truly friendly service and bright rooms draped with thick carpets invite long, lingering meals. Vegetarians come from miles around for the sautéed pumpkin topped with yogurt, spicy carrots spread over fragrant rice and rich eggplant puree. Plenty of meat and fish dishes flesh out the choices. And the baklava – well, it just melts on your tongue.
☎ 212-734-3791
🖳 www.pamirrestaurant.com ✉ 1437 Second Ave
🕑 dinner 🚇 6 to 77th St
🚸 for early dinner Ⓥ

Payard (2, D5) $$$
French
Everyone first came to know Payard as a purveyor of all that is chocolate, but now that it's a patisserie *and* a bistro, dining there can include potato tourte layered with goat's-milk brie or sautéed skate with curried cauliflower purée. And then come the killer desserts!
☎ 212-717-5252
🖳 www.payard.com
✉ 1032 Lexington Ave 🕑 lunch & dinner Mon-Sat 🚇 6 to 77th St
🚹 fair 🚸

Constant Cravings
Late-night dining is common enough in New York, but if you're talking the wee hours, here are a few places you can be sure will be open:
- **Bereket** (3, E5; 187 E Houston St; $) Great Turkish and Middle Eastern food that's available at all hours.
- **Kang Su** (3, C2; 1250 Broadway at 32nd St; $–$$) The best Korean BBQ in town, even at 4am.
- **Mamouns** (3, C5; 119 MacDougal St; $) Unbeatable falafel sandwiches keep this place busy 24-7.
- **Pigalle** (2, B8; 790 Eighth Ave; $) Located in the Day's Inn, this tin-pressed bistro has all the basics for unbeatable prices.
- **Veselka** (3, D4; 144 Second Ave; $) This late-night spot has borscht to perk you right up.

UPPER WEST SIDE

A (2, B1) $–$$
Caribbean fusion
Spicy jerk chicken supported by mango salsa and steak with pineapple rings are two typical fruit-driven mains from A, a casual hangout just on the Morningside Heights border. It's so tiny you'll have to squeeze in but everybody's happy to make room. No alcohol sold but you can BYOB.
☎ 212-531-1643 ✉ 947 Columbus Ave btwn 106th & 107th Sts ☽ dinner Tue-Sat ⊕ B, C to 103 St ♿

Awash (2, B1) $–$$
Ethiopian
Just a few steps away from St John the Divine cathedral is Awash, a neighborhood favorite that serves great Ethiopian combo stews of lamb or chicken with carrots and green beans, wiped up with spongy *injera* (a sourdough-like flat bread). Most of the dishes are meat-based but there's a sizable all-veggie platter that's been vetted for vegans.
☎ 212-961-1416 ✉ 947 Amsterdam Ave ☽ lunch, dinner ⊕ 1, 9 to 110th St ♿ fair ♿ V

'Cesca (2, B5) $$
Italian
Earthy terra-cotta colors and high-backed booths make 'Cesca a congenial place to gather, with the added plus of delicious Italian cooking. Parmigiano fritters and marinated baby artichokes are tasty appetizers, while the swordfish edged with caponata is a typical main. Wonderful wines available by the glass, which you can take at the bar with nibbles.
☎ 212-787-6300 ⬚ www.cescanyc.com ✉ 164 W 75th St ☽ lunch, Mon-Fri, dinner ⊕ 1, 2, 3, 9 to 72nd St ♿ fair

Jean Georges (2, C6) $$$$
French
Jean-Georges Vongerichten's creations are simply awe-inspiring, as is the service at this elegant, spare restaurant. Waiters are so in tune with your needs it seems they can hear your thoughts. Once the food starts coming – butternut squash soup, lobster with Thai herbs, passion fruit sorbet – you'll see why this restaurant consistently wins raves.
☎ 212-299-3900 ⬚ http://jean-georges.com ✉ 1 Central Park West ☽ lunch & dinner Mon-Fri, dinner Sat ⊕ 1, 9, A, B, C, D at 59th St/Columbus Circle

Ouest (2, B4) $$$
American/French
Owned by Tom Valenti, the same chef who owns 'Cesca, this sophisticated eatery has put the Upper West Side on the foodie map. The lively, upscale ambience and eclectic menu – featuring braised lamb shank and pan-roasted sturgeon with risotto – mean this restaurant is in town for good.
☎ 212-580-8700 ⬚ www.ouestny.com ✉ 2315 Broadway at 84th St ☽ dinner ⊕ 1, 9 to 86th St

Picholine (2, B6) $$$$
French/Mediterranean
Chef Terrance Brennan has created a little haven of country cooking on the Upper West Side, matching salmon caponata with earthy vegetable terrines and seven-hour lamb shank with light and airy risottos.
☎ 212-724-8585 ✉ 35 W 64th St ☽ lunch Sat only, dinner ⊕ 1, 9 to 66th St

Rooms With a View
- **Terrace in the Sky** (1, B3; 400 W 119th St; $$$$) This offers spectacular wraparound views of everything south of Harlem.
- **Hotel Metro Rooftop Bar** (2, C9; 45 W 35th St; $) An after-work crowd gathers to dance, drink and watch the setting sun reflect off the Empire State Building.
- **Rainbow Grill** (2, C8; Rockefeller Center; $$$) Open at 5pm every day with great views from the 65th floor.
- **Iris B Cantor Garden** (2, D4; Metropolitan Museum; $$) From April to October this rooftop café is an artistic retreat.

HARLEM/MORNINGSIDE HEIGHTS

Amy Ruth's Home-Style Southern Cuisine (1, C3) $$
Southern soul
Locals know that Amy Ruth's – using recipes from the owner's grandmother – has all the best soul food standards like candied yams, smoked ham, corn pudding, fried okra and more. Waffles are a house specialty, coming with strawberry, blueberry, smothered in sautéed apples, or paired with fried chicken.
☎ 212-280-8779 ⌨ http ://amyruthsrestaurant.com
✉ 113 W 116th St
⏱ breakfast, lunch & dinner Sun-Thu, 24hr Fri & Sat
🚇 2, 3 to 116th St ♿

Miss Mamie's Spoonbread Too (2, B1) $$
Southern Soul
More of a Harlem institution than the Apollo Theater, everyone from Angela Bassett to Mike Tyson to Bill Clinton has dropped in to Mamie's. Owner Norma Jean Darden's family has been serving homemade potato salad, fried okra, mac-and-cheese, short ribs and deep-fried chicken for generations. Miss Maude's Spoonbread Too has the same food, just further uptown (547 Lenox Ave).
☎ 212-865-6744 ⌨ http ://spoonbreadinc.com
✉ 366 W 110th St
⏱ lunch & dinner Mon-Fri, brunch & dinner Sat & Sun
🚇 B, C to 110th St ♿

Native (1, C3) $–$$
French Moroccan/Caribbean
Native prefers grilling to deep-frying, so dishes like cumin-flecked fried chicken,

The food is hot and the waiters are cool at Miss Mamie's

plantain fritters, red curry coconut shrimp and pan-seared catfish are served flaky and light. It's one of the newer offerings on the young Harlem scene.
☎ 212-665-2525 ✉ 161 Lenox Ave ⏱ dinner
🚇 2, 3 to 116th St ♿

Orbit (1, E3) $$
Eclectic
It's rare to find a place with exposed brick walls, hand-painted tables and a massive mural of Marilyn Monroe in rugged East Harlem. Orbit also has live jazz, blues or Brazilian vocalists nightly along with a mixed-bag of festive meal options, including everything from roasted duck rolls and leafy dark greens to chicken pot pie and steak au poivre.
☎ 212-348-7818 ⌨ http ://orbiteastharlem.com
✉ 2257 First Ave
⏱ lunch & dinner Mon-Fri, brunch & dinner Sat & Sun 🚇 6 to 116th St ♿

Settepani's (1, C3) $
Italian/American
One of the new breed of Harlem cafés that are springing up all over, Set-

tepani's is attractive, bright and staffed by an amiable group of African immigrants, most of them students at nearby Columbia University. The coffee is good, as are the sandwiches, quiches and soups, but most people come to chat over dessert, especially the thick, rich carrot and chocolate cakes.
☎ 917-492-4806
⌨ www.settepani.com
✉ 196 Lenox Ave
⏱ lunch, dinner 🚇 2, 3 to 125th St ♿ good ♿ Ⓥ

Sylvia's (1, C2) $$
Southern soul
Open since 1962, this famous Harlem eatery is busy with tour buses, working-class residents and students from Columbia University. Original owner Sylvia Woods still steps into the kitchen herself some days, one of a slew who help to churn out massive portions of buttery collards, fried catfish and excellent banana pudding.
☎ 212-996-0660
⌨ www.sylviassoulfood .com ✉ 328 Lenox Ave
⏱ breakfast, lunch & dinner 🚇 2, 3 to 125th St ♿ fair ♿

BROOKLYN

Alma (6, A4) $$
Mexican

Perfection in three parts: a mellow bar on the ground floor, dramatic dining space in the middle and a marvelous roof garden on top with sweeping views of the Manhattan skyline. Mexican fusion cuisine like spice-rubbed tuna, grilled-veggie fajitas, succulent seviche and magical margaritas make the trek worthwhile.
☎ 718-643-5400 ✉ 187 Columbia St at DeGraw St ⏱ lunch, dinner ⊖ F, G to Bergen ♿

Blue Ribbon Brooklyn (6, A4) $$
American/Seafood

Owned and run by the same brothers who created Blue Ribbon (p67) in Manhattan (and Blue Ribbon Bakery and Blue Ribbon Sushi), this Brooklyn version follows the usual pattern of eccentric comfort food, bolstered by seafood dishes like surf'n'turf and shrimp gumbo. It's great for kids, with lots of dishes they like.
☎ 718-840-0404 🖥 www.blueribbonres taurants.com ✉ 280

Fifth Ave, Prospect Hts/Park Slope ⏱ dinner Mon-Sat, brunch & dinner Sun ⊖ M, R to Union St, F, M, R to Fourth Ave-9th St ♿ very kid friendly

Grimaldi's (6, A4) $
Pizza

Grimaldi's was wildly popular before Dumbo (Down Under the Manhattan Bridge Overpass) was even an acronym. The perfect crusts and spicy sauces, topped with bubbling cheeses of all types, keep customers coming. If the 'no reservations' policy creates long lines sometimes, nobody's complaining.
☎ 718-858-4300 🖥 http ://grimaldisbrooklyn.com ✉ 19 Old Fulton St ⏱ lunch, dinner ⊖ A, C to High St ♿ fair ♿ V

Junior's (6, A4) $
Diner

Constant foot traffic through the doors speaks to Junior's popularity. People come at all hours of the day for fist-sized burgers, onion rings and other typical diner fare, but everything pales next to the creamy smooth richness of its delectable

cheesecake. There's a Junior's in Grand Central Terminal with similar fare.
☎ 718-852-5257 ✉ 386 Flatbush Ave near DeKalb Ave ⏱ breakfast, lunch & dinner ⊖ 2, 3, 4 to Nevins St ♿ fair ♿

Peter Luger (6, A4) $$
Steakhouse

There are certain things everybody knows about Peter Luger: there will be a wait even though you made a reservation, your waiter will be harried (but friendly), and whatever steak (or fish or chicken) you ultimately decide upon will be tender, juicy and made just the way you like it. It will be a legendary experience, and you will want to come back. Cash only and definitely book in advance.
☎ 718-387-7400 🖥 www.peterluger.com ✉ 178 Broadway ⏱ lunch, dinner ⊖ J, M, Z to Marcy Ave ♿ fair ♿

River Café (6, A4) $$$$
American

With its beautiful views from under the Manhattan Bridge the excellent food here is often overlooked. It's perfectly matched to the stellar setting: oysters wrapped in fruitwood-smoked salmon, or the scallop seviche with sea beans and coriander. And the desserts will make you close your eyes with pleasure.
☎ 718-522-5200 🖥 www.rivercafé.com ✉ 1 Water St ⏱ dinner ⊖ A, C to High St-Brooklyn Bridge ♿

River Café – definitely worth a trip to Brooklyn

Entertainment

The Big Apple is especially juicy when it comes to having fun. It's a hard-working town, for sure, but New Yorkers like to play as much as anybody else (and maybe more). There's literally always something on, be it experimental theater on the Lower East Side, world-class ballet in Lincoln Center or an alternative rock fest in Brooklyn. For drinking and old-fashioned bar-hopping, the East Village is your best bet, thanks to its very high bar-to-people ratio. Live music of the underground/experimental ilk is more generally found in the Lower East Side clubs (particularly along East Houston St) and in Greenwich Village. The Meatpacking District is the dernier cri in expensive clubbing, while comedy clubs cluster around Union Sq and Times Sq. Little Korea in Midtown attracts a very diverse late-night scene, and although the Upper West and East sides don't offer the kind of cutting edge entertainment you'll find downtown, there's still

A meeting place for film buffs (p86)

plenty of luxurious bars and eateries to lounge in. Harlem's a hot spot for jazz hounds who want something different and there's always a dance party to be found in one of the big name clubs.

To keep track of it all, start with the Sunday and Friday editions of the *New York Times,* as well as the weekly editions of *New York* magazine, *Time Out New York* and the *New Yorker*. The *Village Voice* has good information on dance clubs and a weekly column (*Fly Life*) that runs down where the best DJs are playing. The **Department of Cultural Affairs** (☎ 212-643-7770) has a hotline that lists events and concerts at major museums and other cultural institutions, while **NYC On Stage** (☎ 212-768-1818), a 24-hour information line, publicizes music and dance events. Other good sources include **Clubfone** (☎ 212-777-2582), **All That Chat** (www.talkinbroadway.com/allthatchat/), **NYC Theatre** (www.nyc.com/theater) and **The Broadway Line** (☎ 888-276-2392).

Special Events

January *Three Kings Parade* – Jan 5; kids parade along Fifth Ave to Spanish Harlem
Chinese New Year – fireworks and parades in and around Chinatown
February *Black History Month* – celebrating African-American history and culture
March *St Patrick's Day Parade* – March 17; a huge Irish march down Fifth Ave
May *Long Island City Art Frenzy* – a mid-month arts festival in Queens
Fleet Week – late May; annual gathering of sailors, naval ships and air rescue teams
Tribeca Film Festival – a star-studded indie film festival founded by Robert DeNiro that brings luminaries from all over
June *JVC Jazz Festival* – mid to late June; concerts with top names in jazz in concert halls around town
NY Shakespeare Festival – three months of free performance in Central Park
Puerto Rican Day Parade – the whole city turns out for this march down Broadway
Lesbian and Gay Pride Week – late June sees a parade down Fifth Ave and many other events in Greenwich Village
July *Independence Day* – on July 4 there are celebrations and fireworks throughout the city
Bastille Day – July 14; an all-day and late-night party takes place on Gansevoort St around Florent (p71)
Lincoln Center Festival – month-long performances by international actors, singers and acrobats (includes free events)
Central Park Concerts – under-the-stars performances by the New York Philharmonic and the Metropolitan Opera
August *Harlem Week* – it's supposed to be seven days devoted to Harlem's history and culture, but it's really the whole month
Charlie Parker Jazz Festival (p37) – late August; has outdoor shows in the East Village and Harlem
Howl! Festival – offers an abundance of East Village alternative theater in mid-August
US Open Tennis Tournament – the last week of August is all about the hard court tennis play in Flushing Meadows, Queens
September *Downtown Arts Festival* – visual and performing arts events in Chelsea and Soho over three weeks
West Indian Day Parade – early in September the city's massive Caribbean population holds a huge Brooklyn parade
San Gennaro – in mid-September Little Italy becomes one big festa dedicated to the patron saint of Naples
New York Film Festival – a major film event held at Lincoln Center
October *Halloween Parade* – on October 31st a wild and colorful march starts in Greenwich Village and goes up Sixth Ave
November *New York Marathon* – in early November professional and amateur runners take to the roads
Macy's Thanksgiving Day Parade – on the 4th Thursday of the month (also a national holiday) this parade runs the length of Broadway
Rockefeller Center Christmas Tree Lighting – at the end of November a huge Christmas tree is lit up in Rockefeller Center
December *New Year's Eve* – on December 31st in Times Sq thousands come for the ball drop. There's also a 5 mile run in Central Park and fireworks at South St Seaport

BARS & LOUNGES

2A (3, E5) A bit down at the heels and rough around the edges, 2A (named after the address) has sweeping views down Ave A and one of the city's friendliest two-for-one happy hours (4pm to 8pm Monday to Friday). Open since the 1980s, 2A has recently cleaned up its act, but is still enough of a dive to be interesting.
☎ 212-505-2466 ✉ 25 Ave A at 2nd St ⏱ 4pm-4am ⊕ F, V to Second Ave ♿ no

Absolutely 4th (3, B4)
A sassy newcomer to a rather laid-back corner, Absolutely 4th has bright yellow French windows that fold back to reveal a funky little bar with irresistible allure (which is heightened by high octane cocktails and snazzy appetizers). On karaoke nights (usually Wednesday) students pour in from nearby New York University to prove their singing mettle.
☎ 212-989-9444 ✉ 228 W 4th St ⏱ 4pm-4am ⊕ A, B, C, E, F, V to W 4th St, 1, 9 to Christopher St-Sheridan Sq ♿ fair ♿ no

Apt (3, B4) The entrance is unmarked and the address supposedly a secret, but the word is out on this swanky Meatpacking District locale. Once you enter the long hallway you start to feel like you're in someone's apartment (and that's precisely the point); the vibe is part voyeur, part high school sleepover (but a whole lot

The umbrella in my cocktail was THIS big!

sexier). Drop by for an 'only in New York' experience.
☎ 212-414-4245 🖥 www.aptwebsite.com ✉ 419 W 13th St ⏱ 10pm-4am; upstairs space (6pm-4am) by reservation only ⊕ A, C, E to 14th St ♿ no

Bemelman's Bar (2, D5)
Love is in the air at this old-fashioned bar in the Carlyle Hotel, aided in part by the happily frolicking animals painted on the walls in magnificent murals by former Carlyle resident Ludwig Bemelman. Delicate piano music makes it a perfect place to unwind after a busy city day.
☎ 212-744-1600 🖥 www.thecarlyle.com ✉ Carlyle Hotel 35 E 76th St at Madison Ave 💲 $20 after 9:30pm, $10 at the bar ⏱ noon-2am Mon-Sat, noon to 12:30am Sun ⊕ 6 to 77th St ♿ fair ♿ no

Church Lounge (3, C6)
This spacious lounge in the Tribeca Grand Hotel gets its share of film- and music-

industry stars. Church has a subdued vibe with plush seating and earth-toned décor that on weeknights in particular make it a lovely place to meet for a drink. On the weekends it's a bit busier and louder, but always elegant.
☎ 212-519-6677 🖥 www.tribecagrand.com ✉ Tribeca Grand Hotel 2 Sixth Ave 💲 free ⏱ 7am-1am Mon-Thu, 7am-1:30am Fri & Sat ⊕ A, C, E to Canal St, 1, 9 to Franklin St ♿ fair ♿ no

Tatt-and-hat dude at 2A

Cub Room (3, C5)
A favorite after-work watering hole for Wall Street types, Cub Room's très chic atmosphere is also warm and inviting. Stroll down the elegant hallway like you own it and order up a big martini. Cub Room offers great bar food, plus fabulous views of Soho through its windows.
☎ 212-677-4100 ✉ 131 Sullivan St ⏱ 10am-4am ⊕ 1, 9 to Houston St, C, E to Spring St ♿ no

Flute (3, C3) Bubbly spills from every corner at Flute, which serves an expansive selection of champagnes and sparkling wines. The deep-red lighting, recessed niches with couches (some with curtains) are sensuous and exciting; order some caviar and start snuggling.
☎ 212-529-7870 ⌨ http://flutebar.com ✉ 40 E 20th St/Union Sq ⏱ 5pm-4am Tue-Sat, 5pm-2am Sun & Mon ⊕ 6 to 23rd St ♿ no

Hell (3, B4) Looking slightly sinister with its faux

Serena – where the famous hang

red velvet drapes and dark, glossy bar, Hell is actually anything but. A Meatpacking resident before the 'nabe was hip, Hell has a loyal mixed clientele that enjoys the slightly Goth ambiance and good house music, as well as the devilish mixed drinks. It's worth checking out the bar next door, **Rhone** (☎ 212-367-8440; www.rhonenyc.com), which is a sleek warehouse space with wines by the glass.
☎ 212-727-1666 ✉ 55 Gansevoort St ⏱ 7pm-4am ⊕ 1, 9, 2, 3, A, C, E to 14th St

PJ Clarke's (2, D7) Irish charm and good beer have made PJ Clarke's a fixture on the East Side for over 100 years. It gets more crowded and loud as the night wears on (the Sidecar upstairs has a quieter ambience; reservations suggested) and strangers become instant friends in this boozy atmosphere.
☎ 212-317-1616 ⌨ www.pjclarkes.com ✉ 915 Third Ave at 55th St ⏱ lunch, dinner, open until 4am ⊕ E, V, 6 to 51st St ♿ no

Serena (3, B3) Unobtrusively tucked down a short flight of stairs, Serena isn't your average basement bar. Framed by attractive Moroccan grillwork, the door leads into a room of cool hues and even cooler drinks. The crowd is upscale but relaxed, and the multi-cushioned couches are deeply inviting.
☎ 212-255-4646 ⌨ www.serenanyc.com ✉ Chelsea Hotel 222 W 23rd St ⏱ 6pm-4am Mon-Thu, 7pm-4am Fri & Sat ⊕ C, E, 1, 9 to 23rd St

Flying Solo
New York's not a bad town to be alone in – there is no stigma to eating or drinking with just yourself for company. There are even advantages: you can eat at the bar while larger parties queue for restaurant tables and you can often pick up prime tickets for theater and sporting events simply because you can slot in anywhere. Restaurants where you'll feel comfortable include Schillers (see boxed text on p69) and Ouest (p78). Serena's (this page) is a good bar scene for singles, Cielo (opposite) on Monday night is the easiest club to visit alone and 55 Bar (p93) is the nicest jazz-for-one spot.

CLUBS

Cheetah (3, C3) Nights vary between hip-hop and house music, with a gay/straight friendly crowd and anything goes attitude. The dancing gets sweaty and unselfconscious and for those who can really feel a groove, there's a stage upstairs.
☎ 212-206-7770 ✉ 12 W 21st St ⏱ 11pm-4am Mon, 10pm-4am Tue-Sun ⊖ 6, N, R to 23rd St ♿ no

Cielo (3, B4) Any night is good at Cielo's small, clubby space, but Monday is the best night to try and slide past the velvet ropes at the door. Live poets and musicians mingle among the frenzied dancers, and the legendary DJ François K holds sway over the whole scene.
☎ 212-645-5700 ⌨ http://deepspacenyc .com ✉ 18 Little West 12th St ⑤ $10 cover ⏱ 9pm-3am ⊖ 1, 9, A, C, E to 14th St ♿ no

Exit2 (2, B7) Famed DJ Junior Vasquez hosts Earth, his one-of-a-kind spin

party, on Saturday night. The entire club is spread out over multiple floors and each one is a maze of themed rooms with its own type of music. If the throng starts to get to you, head upstairs to the roof garden.
☎ 212-582-8282 ✉ 610 W 56th St ⑤ $25 ⏱ 9pm-3am ⊖ A, B, C, D, 1, 9 to Columbus Circle ♿ no

Lotus (3, B3) Flickering candles, pulsating music and loads of beautiful people are the norm at Lotus, a three-level club, disco and restaurant that has deep-pocketed New Yorkers jockeying for entrance into its VIP rooms. Resident DJ Angola spins a fresh mix of house and garage from the basement.
☎ 212-243-4420 ⌨ www.lotusnewyork .com ✉ 409 W 14th St ⑤ $15-25 ⏱ 6pm-4am Wed-Sat ⊖ 1, 9, 2, 3, A, C, E to 14th St

Sapphire Lounge (3, D5) Don't hit this place unless you really want to spend

serious time on the dance floor — there's very little furniture to sit on, in any case. The relatively young crowd starts to throw it down around midnight, grooving to hip-hop, dance, reggae and techno. Partners are easily found and exchanged in this dance haven.
☎ 212-777-5153 ⌨ www.sapphirenyc.com ✉ 249 Eldridge St ⑤ $5 ⏱ 7pm-4am ⊖ F, V to Second Ave ♿ no

Spirit (3, A2) Aiming to align a few chakras while entertaining the masses, Spirit has a wellness center on its dance floor where you can get some acupuncture on that sore knee. Meanwhile an on-site restaurant known as Soul serves up healthy grub — the better to rejuvenate you after an exhausting session with one of Spirit's excellent DJs.
☎ 212-268-9477 ⌨ www.spiritnewyork .com ✉ 530 W 27th St ⑤ $10 ⏱ 10pm-4am Fri & Sat ⊖ 1, 9, A, C to 23rd St

Watch the sunset at Cielo

CINEMAS

Angelika Film Center (3, C5) Angelika specializes in foreign and independent films and has some quirky charms (the rumble of the nearby subway during screenings, for example). But the roomy café is a great place to meet and the beauty of its Stanford White–designed beaux arts building undeniable. ☎ 212-995-2000 🖥 www.angelikafilm center.com ✉ 18 W Houston St at Mercer St 💲 $12 🕑 matinee & evening films shown ⊖ B, D, F, V to Broadway-Lafayette St

Landmark Sunshine Cinema (3, D5) Built in the late 1800s, Sunshine Cinema used to be a Yiddish vaudeville house until it closed in the 1950s. It reopened as a movie theater in 2001 with comfy chairs, great sightlines, a Japanese rock garden and an official poster. It's a beautiful addition to the neighborhood and a great place to catch a flick. ☎ 212-358-7709 ✉ 143 E Houston St 💲 $10

🕑 early matinees & evening shows ⊖ F, V to Lower East Side-Second Ave

Loews Lincoln Sq (2, B6) A posh, eight-story IMAX theater is the centerpiece of this Upper West Side multiplex cinema. The IMAX theater offers several different films, both 3D and regular. Most are new releases straight from Hollywood but the occasional indie production sneaks in. It's also very popular, so get tickets early. ☎ 212-336-5000 🖥 www.enjoytheshow .com ✉ 1992 Broadway at 68th St 💲 $10 🕑 matinee & evening shows ⊖ 1, 2, 3, 9 to 72 St 👍 fair 👶

Revival Theaters

Anthology Film Archives (3, D5) This non-profit organization screens all the best low-budget European films and fringe works from around the world, along with classic revivals and documentaries about film. It also hosts various festivals, like the 'World

of Werner' and the Underground Film Festival (which it sponsors each winter). ☎ 212-505-5181 🖥 www.anthology filmarchives.org ✉ 32 Second Ave at 2nd St 💲 $5 🕑 matinees & evening shows starting in early afternoon ⊖ F, V to Lower East Side-Second Ave

Cinema Classics (3, D4) Grab a coffee at the bar and then slide into the tiny theater to catch a film noir classic, or rarely played movies like *The Name of the Rose*. Of course Woody's a big favorite and *Annie Hall* seems to run every few weeks. For the price, it can't be beat. ☎ 212-677-5368 🖥 www.cinemaclassics .com ✉ 332 E 12th St btwn First Ave & Ave A 💲 $8 🕑 matinees & evening shows starting at 11am ⊖ L to Ave A

Film Forum (3, C5) Frequently showing retrospectives of particular artists, like Fellini or Truffaut, and consistently bringing great movies back from the grave, Film Forum is a favorite place for celluloid buffs. Tickets – even to the most obscure flicks – tend to go fast. Buy in advance when possible. ☎ 212-727-8110 🖥 www.filmforum.com ✉ 209 W Houston St btwn Varick St & Sixth Ave 💲 $12 🕑 matinees & evening shows ⊖ 1, 9 to Houston St

Cinema Under the Stars

Bryant Park (2, C9; ☎ 212-768-4242; www.bryant park.org; Sixth Ave btwn E 40th & 42nd Sts) is famous for its Monday night Film Series that projects both modern and classic films onto a massive screen that goes up every June on the west side of the tree-lined patch of green. Folks show up as early as 3:30pm to get a good spot for the 9pm kick off; recent screenings included *Whatever Happened to Baby Jane*, *Sleepless In Seattle* and *Breakfast at Tiffany's*.

THEATERS

Abrons Art Center (3, E6) This venerable cultural hub has three theaters, the largest being the Harry De Jur Playhouse (a national landmark), which has its own lobby, fixed seats on a rise, a large, deep stage and good visibility. Notable productions have ranged from the US premiere of Mozart's opera *The Emperor's Dream* to shows by The Urban Youth Theater, a troupe immortalized in the documentary *Bones of Our Ancestors*.
☎ 212-598-0400
🖳 www.henrystreet.org
✉ 466 Grand St 🚇 A, C, E to Canal Street-6th Ave

Astor Place Theater (3, D4) Home to the infamous Blue Man Group, this subterranean theater likes to feature interactive avant-garde groups. Expect all sorts of crazy behavior, like toilet paper streaming down from the ceiling.
☎ 212-254-4370
🖳 www.blueman.com
✉ 434 Lafayette St btwn W 4th St & Astor Pl 🚇 R to 8th St-NYU, 6 to Astor Pl

Cherry Lane Theatre (3, B5) A theater with a distinctive charm hidden in the West Village, Cherry Lane has a long and distinguished history. It was started by poet Edna St Vincent Millay and has been home to long-running shows like Sam Shepard's *True West* and Joe Orton's *Entertaining Mr Sloane*.
☎ 212-989-2020
🖳 www.cherrylanethea

On the prowl at the New Amsterdam Theatre in Times Sq

tre.com ✉ 38 Commerce St 🚇 1, 9 to Christopher St-Sheridan Sq

Circle in the Sq Theater (2, C8) Eugene O'Neill's *The Iceman Cometh* was shown at the original Circle in the Sq premises (159 Bleecker St) and new digs uptown haven't softened this theater's sharp eye for talent. It recently exhumed Tennessee Williams' *Not About Nightingales* to great critical acclaim.
☎ 212-307-2705
🖳 www.circlesquare.org
✉ 1633 Broadway at 50th St 🚇 1, 9 to 50th St

Joseph Papp Public Theater (3, D4) Every summer the Papp presents its fabulous Shakespeare in the Park productions at Central Park's Delacorte Theater. Pulitzer-prize winner Suzann-Lori Parks' works all show here, and Meryl Streep and Kevin Kline are two of the many stars who stop by regularly.
☎ 212-260-2400
🖳 www.publictheater .org ✉ 425 Lafayette St

btwn E 4th St & Astor Pl 🚇 N, R to 8th St-NYU, 6 to Astor Pl

Majestic Theater (2, C8) A powerhouse theater that's best known for showing *Carousel*, *South Pacific* and *Camelot* with Julie Andrews, the Majestic has also shown Andrew Lloyd Webber's blockbuster hit *Phantom of the Opera* for about 20 years now – and it's still going strong! Sightlines from just about every seat are excellent.
☎ 212-239-6200
🖳 www.majestic-theater.net ✉ 247 W 44th St at Eighth Ave 🚇 any train to 42nd St-Times Sq-Port Authority

New Amsterdam Theater (2, C8) Recently restored to its full glory, visitors now pass through the gorgeous art deco entrance into an art nouveau interior of carved and painted plaster, carved stone, carved wood, murals and tiles – all of which evoke early-20th-century theater-going.
☎ 212-282-2900
🖳 www.newamster

Central Park SummerStage

This annual series of mostly free concerts, dance performances and readings (www.summerstage .org) takes place at Rumsey Playfield in the center of the park. Only the annual blockbuster benefit concerts charge admission. Access to shows, via the park's Fifth Ave and 69th St entrance, is on a first-come, first-served basis. Ani DiFranco, De La Soul, Elvis Costello, Sonic Youth and Wilco have all sung in Central Park.

damtheater.net ✉ 214 W 42nd St at Seventh Ave ☽ box office walk-in service: 10:00am-8:30pm Mon-Sat, 11am-7pm Sun ⊕ any train to 42nd St-Times Sq/Port Authority ⚒

New Victory Theater (2, C8) New York's ultimate theater for kids and families, presenting the world's best theater, circus, dance, comedy, music and puppetry.

☎ 646-223-3020 ⌨ www.newvictory.org ✉ 209 W 42nd St btwn Broadway & Eighth Ave ⊕ any train to 42nd St-Times Sq/Port Authority ⚒

Orpheum (3, D4) Formerly a Yiddish theatre in the beginning of the 20th century, the Orpheum feeds off creative East Village energy and features off-beat shows like the highly popular musical *Little Shop of Horrors* (now

on Broadway). Currently it's home to 'Stomp,' a dance-happy beat fest.
☎ 212-477-2477 ⌨ www.stomponline .com ✉ 126 Second Ave at 8th St ⊕ 6 to Astor Pl

Winter Garden Theater (2, C7) You'd never guess this building used to be a horse exchange, especially now that the interior has been revamped, remodeled and revitalized. For a brief period, it showed Warner Bros movies but returned to its live performance roots in 1964 with *Funny Girl,* which ran for 1348 performances. Similarly successful shows followed, such as *Auntie Mame* with Bea Arthur.
⌨ www.wintergarden -theater.com ✉ 1634 Broadway at 50th St ☽ box office 10am-8pm Mon-Sat ⊕ N, R to 49th St

COMEDY & CABARET

Comedy

Comedy Cellar (3, C5) This venerable Greenwich Village club has seen quite a few careers come and go over the years, and is still filled nightly with wanna-bes, has-beens and hot-for-the-moment comics. There's always the possibility of a celebrity drop-in; cast members of Saturday Night Live like to test out new material here.
☎ 212-254-3480 ⌨ www.comedycellar .com ✉ 117 MacDougal St btwn 3rd & Bleecker Sts $ $15 with 2 item min ☽ shows start at 9pm Sun-Fri, 7:30pm Sat

⊕ A, C, E, F, V, S to W 4th St ⚒ no

Gotham Comedy Club (3, C3) Don't break out your heckling skills here; these performers are fiercely witty. The elegant Flatiron District club has shows like Comedy Salsa, Sketch Comedy Mondays and New Talent Night run during the week. The last Thursday of the month is Homocomicus, a comedy series dedicated to queer comics.
☎ 212-367-9000 ⌨ www.gothamcomedy club.com ✉ 34 W 22nd St btwn Fifth & Sixth Aves

$ $10.00 cover with 2 drink min Sun-Thu, $16 with 2 drink min Fri & Sat ☽ show starts at 8:30pm Sun-Thu, 8:30pm, 10:30pm & 12:30am Fri & Sat ⊕ F, V, R, W to 23rd St

Ha! Comedy Club in NYC (2, B8) One of the few comedy clubs that welcomes children (over 13 accompanied by an adult), Ha! does four shows a night in two different rooms. Award-winning hosts, hungry beginners and nationally known veterans deliver a wide variety of material and performance at any given show.

☎ 212-977-3884

🖳 www.hacomedynyc
.com ✉ 369 W 46th St

💲 $15 with 2 drink min

🕙 shows start at 6:30pm

🕒 any train to 42nd St-
Times Sq 🕭 fair 🕭

Laugh Factory (2, C8) With
more than 300 plush seats
on a busy Times Sq corner,
the Laugh Factory routinely
pulls in big headliners. It's
not hard to fill seats when
Chris Rock is in town. Regular
nights feature new talent and
the long-running Wendy Williams Comedy Experience.

☎ 212-586-7829

🖳 www.laughfactory
.com ✉ 303 W 42nd St
at Eighth Ave 💲 $15-
40 with 2 drink min

🕙 shows start at 8pm

🕒 any train to 42nd
St-Times Sq/Port Authority

Laugh Lounge (3, E5)
Regular comedy shows pack
'em in Thursday to Friday,
but it's the Comedy Night
Competitions, when two
comedians compete for
audience laughs, that really
get things going at this
Lower East Side funny bar.
Another big hit is Cringe
Humor Comedy Show,
featuring some of the crew
from Comedy Central.

☎ 212-614-2500

🖳 www.laughlounge
nyc.com ✉ 151 Essex St

💲 $10-15 with 2 drink
min 🕙 shows start at
8:30pm 🕒 F, V to Lower
East Side-2nd Ave-
Houston St

Parkside Lounge (3, E5)
Providing a much-loved
alternative to the big main-

stream venues, this dive
bar hosts a weekly comedy
show, the Tuesday Night
Train Wreck, which is just
as wild as it sounds. Come
for the humor and stay for
the late-night Happy Hour:
two-for-one drinks from
2am until closing.

☎ 212-673-6270

🖳 www.parksidelounge
.com ✉ 317 E Houston
St at Attorney St 💲 $5

🕙 8:30pm 🕒 F, V to
Lower East Side-Second
Ave 🕭 no

Cabaret

Cafe Carlyle (2, D5) The
legendary Bobby Short
reigns at this swanky spot
located at the Carlyle Hotel,
drawing star-studded
audiences (Tony Bennett
likes the shows here) and
performers – Woody Allen
has been known to play his
clarinet here on Mondays.
And if she's not doing a
Broadway show, Eartha Kitt
does her torch singer act in
January.

☎ 212-744-1600

🖳 www.thecarlyle.com
✉ 35 E 76th St at
Madison Ave 💲 $30 & up

🕙 shows generally start
at 7pm 🕒 6 to 77th St
🕭 good 🕭

Le Scandal (3, C2) Every
Saturday night The Cutting
Room – owned by Chris
Noth (Mr Big in *Sex and the
City*) and his old college
buddy – hosts Le Scandal, a
cabaret event that includes
the lost art of burlesque
performance. See some of
New York's bawdiest singers
and dancers whoop it up!

☎ 212-691-1900

🖳 www.thecutting
roomnyc.com ✉ 19 W
24th St btwn Sixth Ave
& Broadway 💲 from $5

🕙 hrs vary depending on
show 🕒 6, N, R to 23rd
St 🕭 fair 🕭 no

The Oak Room (2, C8)
Order a martini, settle in
and get the Dorothy Parker
vibe at this Algonquin piano
lounge, where crooners put
a modern twist on Porter,
Gershwin, Kern and Berlin.
The Oak Room is known for
launching the careers of
Harry Connick Jr, Diane Krall
and other hotshots.

☎ 212-840-6800

🖳 www.algonquinhotel
.com ✉ 59 W 44th St
btwn Fifth & Sixth Aves

💲 shows from $30; no
cover charge 🕙 shows
start at 9pm 🕒 B, D, F, V
to 42nd St-Bryant Park

Half-Price Broadway

If you get a sudden urge for a Broadway show, run
to a **TKTS** (www.tdf.org/tkts/) booth and snap up a
bargain deal on cut-rate, same-day tickets to Broadway and off-Broadway musicals and dramas. Tickets
sell at either 25% or 50% off regular box-office rates,
plus a $3 convenience fee. Booths are in Times Sq at
47th St and Broadway and at South St Seaport at
199 Water St between John and Front Sts. Cash or
traveler's checks only.

CLASSICAL MUSIC & OPERA

Amato Opera Theater

(3, D5) *Die Fledermaus*, *The Marriage of Figaro* and *La Bohème* are just a few of the classics put on without a surfeit of glitz or glamour at this no-nonsense theater on the edge of the East Village.

☎ 212-228-8200
🖥 www.amato.org
✉ 319 Bowery at 4th St
Ⓔ 6 to Astor Pl

Carnegie Hall (2, C7)

Many of the world's premier soloists and ensembles give recitals in Carnegie Hall's Isaac Stern Auditorium, the 2804-seat main hall. The legendary hall is visually and acoustically brilliant, as well as enormously tall. Carnegie Hall hosts visiting philharmonics, the New York Pops orchestra and various world-music performers, including Cesaria Evora and Sweet Honey In the Rock.

☎ 212-247-7800
🖥 www.carnegiehall.
org ✉ 154 W 57th St at
Seventh Ave Ⓔ N, R, Q,
W to 57th St

Lincoln Center (2, B6)

There's much more to be heard here than the New York Philharmonic – although that's the name that continues to define Lincoln Center. Year-round shows bring diverse classical stylings, and the occasional visiting opera tackles Prokofiev and Mussorgsky. Tickets can be purchased through **Center Charge** (☎ 212-721-6500). **Alice Tully Hall** (☎ 212-721-6500), meanwhile, is home to the American Symphony Orchestra and the Little Orchestra Society.

☎ 212-875-5900
🖥 www.newyorkphil
harmonic.org ✉ Lincoln
Center Plaza, Broadway at
W 64th St Ⓔ 1, 9 to 66th
St-Lincoln Center

Metropolitan Opera House (2, B6)

Mixing classic and premier performances, the Met is at its best when stars like Renee Fleming and Plácido Domingo take to the stage. Tickets can go up to $200, but start at $55 for lesser-knowns. The $12 standing-room tickets (one of NY's greatest bargains) go on sale at 10am on Saturday for the following week's performances.

☎ 212-362-6000
🖥 www.metopera.org
✉ Lincoln Center, W
64th St at Amsterdam Ave
Ⓔ 1, 9 to 66th St-Lincoln
Center

New York State Theater

(2, B6) Philip-Johnson designed New York City Opera's performance space, which performs new works, overlooked operas and reworked old standards. The split season runs for a few weeks in early autumn and again in early to late spring.

☎ 212-870-5630
🖥 www.nycopera.com
✉ Lincoln Center,
Broadway at 65th Ⓔ 1, 9
to 66th St-Lincoln Center

Town Hall (2, D8)

Town Hall was designed with democratic principles in mind in the early 1900s – box seats and those with partially obstructed views were eliminated (not a bad seat in the house) and the acoustics stunned everyone when first heard. Tours on its history and famous performances are given daily and are well worth the time.

☎ 212-840-2824
🖥 www.the-townhall
-nyc.org ✉ 123 W 43rd
St at Sixth Ave ⏲ 10am-
6pm, closed August, open
for tours Ⓔ B, D, F, V to
42nd St-Bryant Park

Come to Lincoln Center for symphonic harmonies

DANCE

Joyce Theater (3, B3) An offbeat, intimate venue in Chelsea with clean sight-lines from every corner, the Joyce is blessed with annual visits from Merce Cunning-ham and Pilobolus dance companies, which can be comfortably seen from any of the renovated theater's 470 seats.
☎ 212-242-0800
🖳 www.joyce.org
✉ 175 Eighth Ave at W 19th St 🜨 A, C, E to 14th St

New York State Theater (2, B6) The New York City Ballet, established by Lincoln Kirstein and George Balanchine in 1948, features a varied season of pre-mieres and revivals, always including a production of *The Nutcracker* during the Christmas holidays. Discounts available for stu-dents; call the student-rush hotline (☎ 212-870-7766).
☎ 212-870-5570
🖳 www.nycballet.com
✉ Lincoln Center, Broad-way at 63rd 🜨 1, 9 to 66th St-Lincoln Center

> ## Won't You Come Home Alvin Ailey
> After years of performing at various host theat-ers, the renowned **Alvin Ailey American Dance Theater** (☎ 212-767-0590; www.alvinailey.org; W 55th St at Ninth Ave; C, E to 50th St) has moved into its own 77,000-sq-ft home on the West Side. The glass-cube structure contains 12 dance studios, a black box theater, costume shop, concession area, physical therapy center, administrative offices and the Ailey School.

ROCK, HIP HOP & INDIE

Anatomy Bar (3, E4) Big pieces of local art hang on the walls while a DJ spins hip-hop and laid-back house from a booth in the back. A mixed crowd of twenty- and thirty-somethings play pool and lounge on the many couches against the walls. In summer, there's a garden in back. From Tuesday to Thursday the DJ plays indie and hip-hop specifically.
☎ 212-995-8889
🖳 http://anatomybar andlounge.com ✉ 511 E 6th St 🕐 6pm-4am 🜨 6 to Astor Pl, F, V to Second Ave, N, R, W to 8th St

Beacon Theater (2, B5) An Upper West Side venue with a lot of cool atmosphere, the Beacon is perfect for folks who want to see shows in a more intimate environment than that of a big concert arena. Moby, Aimee Mann and the Allman Brothers have all played the stage.
☎ 212-496-7070
✉ 2124 Broadway btwn 74th & 75th Sts 🕐 hrs vary 🜨 1, 2, 3, 9 to 72nd St

Bowery Ballroom (3, D5) A big favorite since it opened in 1998, Bowery Ballroom is as esteemed for its darkly swank, well-stocked bar as its musical acts. Jonathan Richman, American Music Club and the Delgados have all recently played here.
☎ 212-533-2111
🖳 www.boweryball room.com ✉ 6 Delancey St 🕐 hrs vary 🜨 6 Delancey St at Bowery, J, M to Bowery

CBGB (3, D5) The birth-place of the punk-rock revo-lution, this dark little den is still going strong after nearly three decades. Even though the name stands for 'Country, Bluegrass and Blues,' rock is what's usually heard. Blondie, the Talking Heads and the Ramones sweated through legendary sets here, and all types of up-and-comers still grace the stage.
☎ 212-982-4052
🖳 www.cbgb.com
✉ 315 Bowery btwn E 1st & 2nd Sts 💲 free before band starts 🕐 6pm-4am 🜨 6 to Bleecker St

Continental (3, D4) With its blasted interior and thrash-core clientele, Con-tinental is, quite proudly, a rock-and-roll dump. A dump blessed with surprise gigs from the likes of Iggy Pop and Jakob Dylan, that is! It's gritty, dirty and loads of fun. ☎ 212-529-6924 ⌨ www.continental nyc.com ✉ 25 Third Ave at St Marks Pl ⑤ varies ⏱ 4pm-3am ⊙ N, R to 8th St-NYU, 6 to Astor Pl

Joe's Pub (3, D4) Part cabaret, part bar, Joe's Pub is filled with plush red cushioned chairs and attracts some of the most interesting performers in town, from newly-minted icons like Carl Hancock Rux to the irascible Sandra Bernhard. ☎ 212-539-8770 ⌨ www.joespub.com ✉ The Public Theater, 425 Lafayette St btwn Astor Pl & E 4th St ⑤ varies ⏱ 7pm-4am ⊙ R, W to 8th St–NYU (W weekdays only), 6 to Astor Pl

Karma (3, E5) Karma is one of the last places in town that openly ignores the no-smoking law, but it's also popular for the late-

Mercury Lounge, mercury rising

night dancing to stylish DJs spinning funk and house (on certain nights of the week it's all Latin, reggae or hip-hop). The all-day happy hour (10am to 8pm) and delectable bar snacks keep the place crowded well before the dancing begins. ☎ 212-677-3160 ⌨ http://karmanyc.com ✉ 51 First Ave btwn 3rd & 4th Sts ⏱ noon-4am ⊙ F, V to Second Ave

Luna Lounge (3, E5) Rather scruffy and un-prepossessing from the outside, Luna is a mellow bar that attracts garage bands, local musicians and up-and-coming indie darlings every night of the

week. The Strokes, Kid Rock and Madder Rose have all graced the teeny stage here. Monday night is comedy night and it's definitely a hoot! ☎ 212-260-2323 ⌨ http://lunalounge .com ✉ 171 Ludlow St at Stanton St ⑤ varies ⏱ 7:30pm-4am ⊙ F, V to Lower East Side-Second Ave

Mercury Lounge (3, E5) Many a big-name artist paid their dues at Mercury and they are still apt to pop in for a nostalgic evening from time to time (Lou Reed or John Popper, for example). This Lower East Side joint always has something worth hearing and boasts a quality sound system – great for dancing and grooving, and there's a separated bar at front for those who want to talk without straining vocal cords. ☎ 212-260-4700 ⌨ www.mercury loungenyc.com ✉ 217 E Houston St at Essex St ⑤ varies ⏱ 4pm-4am ⊙ F, V to Lower East Side-Second Ave-Houston St

Arthur's Tavern
Everything at **Arthur's** (3, B4; ☎ 212-675-6879; www.arthurstavernnyc.com; 57 Grove St off Seventh Ave; ⏱ 7pm-4am ⊙ 1, 9 to Christopher St) is a little worse for wear, but cram in anyway to hear Frankie Paris and his band cover all sorts of sounds, from Prince to Lynrd Skynrd to Ray Charles to Jane's Addiction. Local musicians regularly stop by to jam and Frankie's generous with the stage. Great live music in a let-your-hair-down kind of place, with no cover and a one-drink-per-set minimum right in the heart of Greenwich Village.

JAZZ, BLUES & WORLD

BB King's Joint (2, C8)
A two-tiered, horseshoe-shaped room in the heart of Times Sq, BB King's has featured names like Merle Haggard and Etta James, and cool secondary bills at the adjacent Lucille's Grill. Classic rockers like Peter Frampton and Blue Öyster Cult as well as R&B legends like Chic and James Brown always do a gig here when they're in town.
☎ 212-997-4144
⌨ www.bbkingblues
.com ✉ 237 W 42 St
$ varies ⏲ 11am-2am
⊕ any train to 42nd St-Times Sq/Port Authority

Birdland (2, B8)
Named for Charlie Parker, or 'Bird,' this jazz club has been turning out big-name acts since 1949, when Theloni-ous Monk, Miles Davis, Stan Getz and others made music and cut records in front of a live audience. Today you're likely to catch the Duke El-lington Orchestra (directed by Paul Mercer Ellington), the James Moody Quartet or Stanley Jordan.
☎ 212-581-3080
⌨ www.birdlandjazz
.com ✉ 315 W 44th St
btwn Eighth & Ninth Aves
$ varies ⏲ afternoon-late ⊕ A, C, E to 42nd St-Port Authority

CHICAGO B.L.U.E.S (3, B3)
This West Village venue hosts visiting blues masters nightly. If you've got a har-monica in your pocket, jump in for Monday night's blues jam, or sit back and listen to the up-and-comers.
☎ 212-924-9755 ✉ 73

Eighth Ave at W 14th St
⊕ A, C, E to 14th St

Copacabana (3, A1)
Setting off a rumba revolution on the West Side, this two-level pink stucco behemoth of a club is packed with after-work revelers looking to let loose and live a lot. Coat check at the entrance, basic salsa lessons (no charge) on the lower level, a free buffet (with paid entrance) and slamming sounds from live bands translate into busy feet – the dance floor gets crowded but there's always room for one more.
☎ 212-239-2672 ✉ 560 W 34th St $ $10 week-nights; $25 weekends
⏲ 7pm-2am
⊕ any train to Herald Sq
♿ fair ♿ no

55 Bar (3, B4)
An unpre-tentious basement gem fa-voring jazz and blues driven by funky, guitar-laden combos that get everyone's feet tapping. 55 Bar has a glow all its own. Spilling music onto a historic corner of the Village (it's next to Stonewall) at all hours, 55

Bar has the best of old and new sounds.
☎ 212-929-9883
⌨ www.55bar.com
✉ 55 Christopher St
btwn W 4th St & Waverly
Pl $ $3-15, incl 2 drinks
⏲ 1pm-4am ⊕ 1, 9 to Christopher St/Sheridan Sq, A, B, C, D, E, F to W 4th St

Jazz Standard (2, D2)
Attached to a great restau-rant, the source of all the steaming plates of pulled-pork sandwiches, pan-fried catfish and beef brisket flying around, the Jazz Standard does fabulous live performances of newcomers and old hands. After dinner and a set you can hang at the bar with the artists.
☎ 212-576-2232
⌨ jazzstandard.com
✉ 116 E 27th St btwn
Park & Lexington Aves
$ varies ⏲ 6pm-3am
⊕ 6 to 28th St

SOBs (3, C5)
SOBs stands for Sounds of Brazil. Samba, Afro-Cuban music, salsa and reggae, both live and on the turntable, get people

King for a night

shaking it on the dance floor. The club hosts dinner shows nightly but it doesn't really start jumping until 2am. Check out the weekly 'Basement Bhangra,' a six-year-old party that's become a mecca for the rapidly growing number of Asian-hip-hop fanatics.
☎ 212-243-4940
🖳 www.sobs.com
✉ 204 Varick St btwn King & Houston Sts
💲 varies ⏱ 6:30pm-3am 🚇 1, 9 to Houston St

Symphony Space (2, B3)
A gem of the upper-Upper West Side, this recently-refurbished concert hall likes world-music concerts. Groups have performed gypsy, Scottish, Indian and Greek music, and GrooveLily also made an appearance.
☎ 212-864-1414
🖳 www.symphony space.org ✉ 2537 Broadway at 95th St 💲 varies ⏱ show times vary 🚇 1, 2, 3, 9 to 96th St

Tonic (3, E5) Tonic garners consistent acclaim for

All That Jazz
The Frederick P Rose Hall Jazz Center in the Time Warner building (2, B7) has three performance spaces, an educational center and the Jazz Hall of Fame. The Rose Theater has 1200 seats, Dizzy's Club has 140 seats, and the Allen Room, with 600 seats, also features a dance floor and a wall of glass with panoramic views of the city. The world's first performing arts center specifically designed for jazz is groovy enough to make Ken Burns and artistic director Wynton Marsalis proud.

avant-garde jazz, rock and electronic acts. Each month, different musicians – including John Zorn, Alan Licht and Arto Lindsay – program different series. Performances are always intimate and from Thursday to Friday the downstairs lounge features DJs entertaining the excess crowd from upstairs.
☎ 212-358-7501
🖳 www.tonicnyc.com
✉ 107 Norfolk St btwn Delancy & Rivington Sts
💲 $8-12 ⏱ 7pm-midnight Sun-Wed, 7pm-3am Thu-Sat 🚇 F to Delancy St

Village Vanguard (3, B4) Possibly the world's most prestigious jazz club, the Vanguard has hosted literally every major star of the past 50 years. It started as a home to spoken word performances and occasionally harkens to its roots, but most of the time it's just smooth, sweet jazz all night long.
☎ 212-255-4037
🖳 www.village vanguard.net ✉ 178 Seventh Ave at W 11th St
💲 $15-40, 2 drink min ⏱ 7pm-1am 🚇 1, 9 to Christopher St-Sheridan Sq

Jazz things up at the Village Vanguard

GAY & LESBIAN NEW YORK CITY

B Bar (3, D4) Come here on Tuesday for Beige, a long-running gay party laden with fashion-industry regulars, who all hang out at the bar and look fabulous.
☎ 212-475-2220
✉ 40 E 4th St $ $15
⏱ 11am-3am ⊕ 6 to Bleecker St

Club Shelter (3, C1) Check out this multi-level space on Saturday, night of the long-running deep-house party, Shelter, with DJ Timmy Regisford. On the same night, Lovergirl packs in lesbian homegirls on a couple of its other floors for a party known more for its cruising than its sounds.
☎ 212-719-4479
🖥 www.clubshelter.com ✉ 20 W 39th St btwn Fifth & Sixth Aves
$ $10-20 ⏱ 9pm-4am ⊕ B, D, F, V to 42 St-Bryant Park

Crobar (3, A2) This brand-new megaclub (sibling to Crobars in Miami and Chicago) caters to a largely suburban crowd on weekends, but holds plenty of queer-tinged bashes with super DJs.
☎ 212-629-9000
🖥 http://crobar.com ✉ 530 W 28th St btwn Tenth & Eleventh Aves
$ $20 ⏱ 11pm-5am ⊕ A, C, E to 34th St-Penn Station

g (3, B3) A simple 'g' hanging in the window indicates that you've arrived at this high-glam but unpretentious bar, where mostly gay

men sip strong drinks and move to the music. A juice bar is hidden in the back.
☎ 212-929-1085
🖥 www.glounge.com ✉ 225 W 19th St btwn Seventh & Eighth Aves
⏱ 4pm-4am ⊕ 1, 9 to 18th St ♿ fair

Opaline (3, E4) This lush lounge becomes Area 10009 on Fridays, when 'It' hosts Amanda Lepore, Sophia Lamar and Dee Finley suck in a queer and queer-friendly crowd for a decadent evening, set to beats from DJs Nita and Formika.
☎ 212-995-8684 ✉ 85 Ave A btwn 5th & 6th Sts
$ $10 ⏱ 5pm-4am ⊕ F, V to Lower East Side-Second Ave

Posh (2, B7) Not at all posh, this gorgeous little place in Hell's Kitchen has a steady stream of gay and lesbian customers accompanied by straight friends. Comfy couches and a spinning DJ add festive touches, while flavorful, fruity drinks are worth the $9.
☎ 212-957-2222 ✉ 405 W 51st St at Ninth Ave
⏱ 4pm-4am ⊕ C, E to 50th St

Starlight Bar & Lounge (3, E4) A funky mix of Chelsea boys and East Village artistes cross paths in this pleasantly overcrowded bar, with room to relax in the back lounge. The all-female bartender crew work the crowd and Sunday night ('Starlette') is widely considered one of the best lesbian events in the city. Wednesday is queer comedy night, hosted by funny man Keith Price.
☎ 212-475-2172
🖥 starlightbarlounge.com ✉ 167 Ave A btwn 10th & 11th Sts $ $10 ⏱ 7pm-3am ⊕ L to First Ave

Wonder Bar (3, E4) Grungily stylish and so very friendly, Wonder Bar is still an all-time favorite gay and lesbian spot in the East Village, which otherwise tends to be a very hetero 'hood. Lots of beer-drinking youth mingle with the gin-and-tonic crowd on weeknights, and on weekends it's packed full of a very mixed crowd.
☎ 212-254-0688 ✉ 505 E 6th St btwn Aves A & B ⏱ 6pm-4am ⊕ F, V to Second Ave

Where the Boys Are

It's not often you can see a man decked out in skin-tight leather dancing on top of a bar talking on his cell phone – but at **Rawhide** (3, B3; ☎ 212-242-9332; 212 Eighth Ave at 21st St; straight and gay) it's practically a nightly occurrence. This Chelsea bar has been pulling out all the stops for nearly two decades now, outliving numerous 'quality of life' initiatives that sought to curtail the fun.

SPORTS

New Yorkers aren't the nation's most rabid sports fans (that honor goes to the residents of Chicago), but they are a close second. Baseball, known as the 'New York game' when its rules were first written in 1846, reigns supreme. The city's pro baseball teams are the extraordinarily successful Yankees (American League), who have won the World Series more than any other franchise, and the ugly duckling Mets (National League). The season runs from April to October. Most sporting events can be booked through Ticketmaster (☎ 212-307-7171).

Two farm teams in the New York Penn League have developed a healthy rivalry and continue to attract big crowds out to Brooklyn and Staten Island for evening and weekend games. The Brooklyn Cyclones and Staten Island Yankees are the Mets–Yankees of the B league.

Basketball, although invented in Massachusetts, is also closely associated with New York. The city's National Basketball Association team is the Knicks – Spike Lee and Woody Allen are big fans. There's strong support for the New York Liberty women's team too. Both teams play at Madison Sq Garden. The New Jersey Nets basketball team may soon be moving to Brooklyn – a new stadium is under development there to house them.

NY Giants football tickets sell out years in advance; season tickets are hotly contested in divorce battles and left to children in wills. Tickets to the somewhat second-tier but popular New York Jets football games are easier to come by. The season runs from September to January; both teams play at the Meadowlands Sports Complex (4, A2) in New Jersey.

Yankee Stadium – where the bases (and seats) are always loaded

The New York Rangers play ice hockey at Madison Sq Garden from October to April. Their rivals, the New York Islanders, play at Nassau Veterans Memorial Coliseum. The best area team, the New Jersey Devils, plays across the Hudson River.

Let's play ball!

The US Open is the year's final Grand Slam tennis event (spanning the Labor Day weekend) at Flushing Meadows. Reserved tickets are only required for Arthur Ashe Stadium, which is sold out months ahead. Day-session ground passes are sold on the morning of each day's play – if you're in line before 9am you might snag one.

Belmont Park is the area's biggest horseracing track. The season runs from May to July.

Sporting Venues

- **Belmont Park** (☎ 516-488-6000; www.nyra.com; Hempstead Turnpike, Elmont, Long Is; LIRR from Penn Station to Belmont) horse racing
- **Giants Stadium** (4, B1; ☎ 201-935-3900; www.meadowlands.com; East Rutherford, NJ; Meadowlands bus from Port Authority) Giants and Jets football, MetroStars soccer, concerts
- **Key Span Park** (☎ 718-449-8497; www.brooklyncyclones.com; 1904 Surf Ave, Brooklyn) minor league baseball
- **Madison Sq Garden** (3, B2; ☎ 465-MSG1; www.thegarden.com; Seventh Ave & W 33rd St; Penn Station) basketball, ice hockey and concerts
- **Nassau Veterans Memorial Coliseum** (☎ 516-794-9300; www.nassaucoliseum.com; 1255 Hempstead Turnpike, Uniondale, Long Is; LIRR to Hempstead, then bus N70-72) ice hockey and NY Saints indoor lacrosse team
- **National Tennis Center** (6, B4; ☎ 718-760-6200, booking 866-673-6849; www.usopen.org; Flushing Meadows-Corona Pk, Queens; 7 to Shea Stadium-Willets Point) tennis
- **Richmond County Bank Ballpark at St George** (☎ 718-720-9265; www.siyanks.com; 75 Richmond Terrace, Staten Island, NY) minor league baseball
- **Shea Stadium** (6, C2; ☎ 718-507-8499; tickets 718-507-8499; www.mets.com; Flushing Meadows, Queens; 7 to Shea Stadium-Willets Point; ferry: NY Waterways ferry from Sth St Seaport, ☎ 800-53-FERRY) home to Mets baseball games
- **Yankee Stadium** (4, A2; Yankees ☎ 718-293-6000; Ticketmaster 307-7171; www.yankees.com; 161st St & River Ave, the Bronx; B (weekdays only), 4, D to 161st St-Yankee Stad; ferry: NY Waterways ferry from Sth St Seaport) home to the Yankees baseball team

Sleeping

Sleek bars, beautiful restaurants, even full-on nightclubs can be found in many Manhattan hotels these days, and New Yorkers like to savor them as much as any visitor. In the see-and-be-seen world of lobbies and lounges you'll likely rub elbows with more than a few locals (and very possibly celebs too). Especially so in the trendy boutique hotels that became all the rage in 1985 and remain immensely popular.

While boutiques may get the most play, there is definitely something here for everyone: the business-class luxury of the Ritz-Carlton (p99), the country charm of the Larchmont Hotel (p102), the trend-setting style of the Hotel Gansevoort (p99) or the budget comfort and character of the Gershwin Hotel (p102).

Finding special rates and discounts is much easier with the Internet. First try **Priceline** (www.priceline.com) and **Hotwire** (www.hotwire.com). **Orbitz** (www.orbitz.com) lets you choose your hotel's star rating and amenities and then gives you several options, as do sites like **Hotels.com** (www.hotels.com), **Hoteldiscounts.com** (www.hotel discounts.com) and **Travelzoo** (www.travelzoo.com), all claiming prices that are up to 70% less than the standard rates. **Just New York Hotels** (www.justnewyorkhotels.com), **New York Deals on Hotels** (www.newyork .dealsonhotels.com), **New York City Hotels Today** (www.newyorkcity hotelstoday.com) and **NYC Hotels** (www.nyc-hotels.net) work the same way, but are focused strictly on NYC. Checking individual hotel's websites is also worth a shot, as several offer special Internet-only deals.

Room Rates

Price ranges indicate the standard rate for one night in a double room.

Deluxe	$300–15,000+
Top End	$300–800
Mid-Range	$100–300 standard rooms; suites from $250–500
Budget	$100 and under

Prices do not include New York's $13.25% hotel sales tax. Prices also fluctuate depending on the season.

Smooth elegance at 60 Thompson (left; p99) and The Time (right; p101)

DELUXE

The Kitano (2, D9) The Kitano has a sleek, hushed Eastern vibe. Rooms are simple and large, featuring futons, wood floors, shoji paper screens and tatami mats. The on-site restaurant is the only one in the city serving Japanese *kaiseki* cuisine (a traditional accompaniment to the Japanese tea ceremony).
☎ 212-885-7000 🖳 www .thekitano.com ✉ 66 Park Ave 🚇 6 to Grand Central Terminal 🚻 fair ✗ Nadaman Habukai

The Mark (2, D5) Discreet and elegant, The Mark calls itself a contemporary sanctuary, and that's pretty close to the truth. The lovely Biedermeier furnishings, antique prints, high-end linens and beautifully detailed decor make you feel like you've stepped miles away from the busy streets. It's also within walking distance to many of the city's best-known museums.
☎ 212-744-4300 🖳 www.themarkhotel .com ✉ 25 E 77th St 🚇 6 to 77th St 🚻 good ✗ Mark's Restaurant 🛗

Ritz Carlton New York, Battery Park (3, C9) Telescopes sit in all the waterside rooms and suites of this 38-story glass-and-brick tower, the better to see the sweeping harbor and city views. The big marble baths (and 'bath-butler' service), goose-down pillows, on-site spa and gym, two top-notch restaurants (with stunning tableside views at Rise) and complimentary downtown car service come together to form an incredibly luxurious experience.
☎ 212-344-0800 🖳 www.ritz-carlton.com ✉ 2 West St at Battery Pl 🚇 1, 9 to South Ferry, 4, 5 to Bowling Green 🚻 good ✗ 2 West, Rise

TOP END

60 Thompson (3, C5) This 100-room gem has a gorgeous rooftop terrace with views of the Empire State Building, an intimate courtyard, and rooms with wrought-iron balconies, down duvets, leather-paneled walls and the custom-designed Thompson Chair. The intimate Thom restaurant is also a winner.
☎ 212-431-0400 🖳 www.60thompson. com ✉ 60 Thompson St btwn Broome & Spring Sts 🚇 C to Spring St-6th Ave 🚻 good ✗ Thom 🛗

The Carlyle (2, D5) This classic is the epitome of old-fashioned luxury: a hushed lobby, antique boudoir chairs and framed English country scenes or Audubon prints in the rooms, some of which have terraces and baby grand pianos.
☎ 212-744-1600 🖳 www.thecarlyle.com ✉ 35 E 76th St btwn Madison & Park Aves 🚇 6 to 77th St-Lexington Ave 🚻 good ✗ Carlyle Cafe

Four Seasons (2, D7) Designed by renowned architect IM Pei, this limestone monolith has 52 floors, all full of spacious rooms with a design that's simple yet deluxe. The blond-wood lobby lounge serves tiered trays of crustless sandwiches for tea, and the bar in the restaurant gets mobbed with upscale after-work drinkers.
☎ 212-758-5700 🖳 www.fourseasons .com/newyorkfs/index .html ✉ 57 E 57th St at Park Ave 🚇 6 to 59th St-Lexington Ave 🚻 fair ✗ Fifty Seven Fifty Seven 🛗

Hotel Gansevoort (3, B4) This 187-room luxury hotel in the trendy Meatpacking District opened in January 2004 and was an instant hit. Could it be the 400-thread-count linens? Hypoallergenic down duvets? Plasma TVs? Steam showers? Yes, yes and oh yes. Also the jaw-dropping views, luscious spa and fitness center, pet-friendly floors and the trendy location.
☎ 212-206-6700 🖳 www.hotelganse voort.com ✉ 18 Ninth Ave at 13th St 🚇 A, C, E to 14th St and 8th Ave 🚻 good ✗ Ono 🛗

Mandarin Oriental New York (2, B7) New York's most opulent option yet is in the newly unveiled Time Warner Center (p34). Amenities range from soaking tubs overlooking the park or the Hudson, flat-screen televisions and an unrivalled, sophisticated style.

☎ 212-885-8800
🖳 www.mandarin oriental.com ✉ 80 Columbus Circle at 60th St ❸ A, B, C, D 1 or 9 to 59th St-Columbus Circle ♿ good ✗ numerous restaurants ⚲

The Mercer (3, C5) It's sleek and grand and so cool that it doesn't even have a sign. The hushed lobby features a library, the excellent restaurant is a destination eatery for discerning locals and the vast loft-like rooms (with flooding sunlight and exposed brick) evoke the once-upon-a-time artist's way the 'hood was formerly known for.

☎ 212-966-6060
🖳 www.mercerhotel .com ✉ 147 Mercer St at Prince St ❸ N, R to Prince St ♿ fair ✗ Mercer Kitchen ⚲

Peninsula (2, D7) Opened in 1904, this grand dame is one of the oldest major hotels in Midtown. The totally renovated space includes an elegant stairway sweeping up from the lobby, and a sprawling spa and athletic club with a sizable pool. The contemporary art nouveau rooms have lots of technological touches.

☎ 212-956-2888, 800-262-9467 🖳 www.new york.peninsula.com ✉ 700 Fifth Ave at 55th St ❸ E, V to Fifth Ave-53rd St ♿ good ✗ Fives, Gotham Bar & Lounge ⚲

MID-RANGE

Algonquin (2, C8) The famed location of Dorothy Parker's Round Table, the Algonquin still attracts visitors with its upscale decor and classic 1902 lobby. It has a 24-hour fitness center, and comfortable (if a bit small) rooms.

☎ 212-840-6800
🖳 www.algonquinhotel .com ✉ 59 W 44th St btwn Fifth & Sixth Aves ❸ F, B, D, V to 42nd

St-Bryant Park ♿ good ✗ Blue Bar ⚲

Casablanca (2, C8) With its North African motifs – tiled floors, bold statues and carved headboards – the Casablanca is both low-key *and* high-class. Nice touches include a complimentary breakfast, all-day snacks and espresso coffee, and free wine and appetizers (weekdays only). The rooms

aren't huge, but the hotel and staff are so charming you hardly notice.

☎ 212-869-1212, 888-922-7225 🖳 www .casablancahotel.com ✉ 147 W 43rd St ❸ any train to Times Sq-42nd St/Port Authority ♿ fair ✗ no

Chelsea Hotel (3, B3) This infamous inn is a literary and cultural landmark brimming

---

How Suite It Is

- The **Tatami Suite** at the Kitano (p99) is tricked out with Japanese paper lanterns, screens, futons and tatami mats. The hotel can even turn this suite into the site of your very own traditional tea ceremony.
- Covering 1000 sq ft, the **Carlyle Suite** at The Carlyle (p99) is a sumptuous option, with antique furniture and its very own grand piano.
- The **Terrace Suite** at the Maritime Hotel (opposite) provides guests with eclectic but comfortable nautical digs enhanced by sweeping Hudson views, private gardens and outdoor showers.

with New York nostalgia. Everyone from Dylan Thomas to Arthur C Clarke has stayed here and it's also where Sid Vicious killed Nancy Spungen. The cheapest rooms have shared bathroom; the most expensive suites have a separate living room, dining area and kitchen. Every room has high ceilings, air-con and its own unique style.
☎ 212-243-3700
🖳 www.hotelchelsea .com ✉ 222 W 23rd St 🕐 C, E to 23rd St-Eighth Ave ✗ no

Chelsea Lodge (3, B3) This landmark brownstone in Chelsea's historic district has compact rooms with hardwood floors, comfy beds and great light. You'll get lots of charm and attention for a reasonable price, as well as a room in the loveliest part of the neighborhood.
☎ 212-243-4499
🖳 www.chelsealodge .com ✉ 318 W 20th St btwn Eighth & Ninth Aves 🕐 C, E to 23rd-Eighth Ave 🛉

Efuru Guest House (1, C3) This beautiful restored brownstone is close to many Harlem attractions. Each of the rooms – Parlor and Garden Studio, and Deluxe Room with semi-private bath – exudes a gracious and winning charm.
☎ 212-961-9855
🖳 www.efuru-nyc.com ✉ 106 W 120th St at Lenox Ave 🕐 2, 3 to 116th St-Lenox Ave

The Library Hotel (2, D8) Each floor in this cleverly themed space is dedicated

'A double room in Philosophy? Certainly.' The Library Hotel

to one of the ten major categories of the Dewey Decimal System. The handsome style here is bookish, too: mahogany paneling, hushed reading rooms and a gentleman's-club atmosphere, thanks largely to its stately 1912 brick mansion home origins.
☎ 212-983-4500
🖳 www.libraryhotel .com ✉ 299 Madison Ave at 41st St 🕐 any train to 42nd St-Grand Central 🚻 fair ✗ Reading Room 🛉

Mansfield Hotel (2, D8) A 1904 building with all its historic elements intact (despite renovations), the Mansfield has cozy rooms with big beds and plush amenities and is in an excellent location. Everything is top of the line, right down to the Belgian linens. The M Bar has a fabulous domed glass-and-lead ceiling.
☎ 212-944-6050
🖳 www.mansfieldhotel .com ✉ 12 W 44th St btwn Fifth & Sixth Aves 🕐 any train to 42nd St-Grand Central Terminal 🚻 fair ✗ M Bar 🛉

Maritime Hotel (3, B3) Portholes dot the white

tower of this marine-themed luxury inn. It feels like an opulent ocean liner, as its 120 rooms, each with its own round window, are compact and teak-paneled; the most expensive quarters feature outdoor showers, a private garden and sweeping Hudson views. An eatery and outdoor cocktail lounge are precious perks.
☎ 212-242-4300
🖳 www.themaritimeho tel.com ✉ 363 W 16th St btwn Eighth & Ninth Aves 🕐 A, C, E to 14th St-Eighth Ave or 1, 2, 3, 9 to 14th St-Seventh Ave 🚻 fair ✗ Matsuri 🛉

The Time (2, C8) This palace of modern design has red, blue and yellow schemes that vary from room to room. The red room, in addition to being crimson, features red candy and a bottled 'red scent' to really make its point. The design is really sumptuous, though, and the lovely lounge downstairs has tapas and a specialty martini.
☎ 212-320-2900
🖳 www.thetimeny.com ✉ 224 W 49th St btwn Broadway & Eighth Ave 🕐 1, 9 to 50th St-Broadway 🚻 good ✗ Oceo, La Gazelle 🛉

BUDGET

Bowery's Whitehouse Hotel (3, D5) Location, location, location! Right on the Bowery, just steps away from some of the best shows, clubs and restaurants, this bare bones (but attractive) option is a big favorite with students and frugal travelers. There are safe, secure private rooms, but no private bathrooms.
☎ 212-477-5623
🖳 www.whitehouseho telofny.com ✉ 340 Bowery ⊙ 6 to Bleecker St

Gershwin (3, C2) This popular and funky spot (half youth hostel, half hotel) is buzzing with original artwork, touring bands and other fabulousness. It has a cool new lobby bar, and sits right next door to the Museum of Sex (p42).
☎ 212-545-8000
🖳 www.gershwinhostel .com ✉ 7 E 27th St at Fifth Ave ⊙ 6 or N to 28th St-Park Ave

Hotel 17 (3, D3) This popular spot has serious character – and that's not

even counting its past as a location for Woody Allen's *Manhattan Murder Mystery* and a Madonna photo shoot. There's an old-fashioned elevator, a cool chandelier in the lobby, vintage wallpaper and worn but chic charm to the small, quiet rooms.
☎ 212-475-2845
🖳 www.hotel17ny.com ✉ 225 E 17th St btwn Second & Third Aves ⊙ any train to 14th St-Union Sq

Jazz on the Park Hostel (2, B1) The recently refurbished Jazz on the Park now looks way too cool for a hostel. Rooms are small, with standard bunks, but there's a beautiful roof deck

and exposed-brick lounge that hosts local jazz acts.
☎ 212-932-1600
🖳 www.jazzhostel.com ✉ 36 W 106th St btwn Central Park West & Manhattan Ave ⊙ any train to 14th St-Union Sq

Larchmont Hotel (3, C4) Cozy and affordable, with shared bathrooms and communal kitchens, the hotel's 52 rooms include sinks and perks such as robes and slippers. It's in a plum spot on a leafy Fifth Ave block.
☎ 212-989-9333
🖳 www.larchmonthotel .com ✉ 27 W 11th St btwn Fifth & Sixth Aves ⊙ any train to 14th St-Union Sq

Staying with Family
Gay-run-and-owned, these charming B&B-type locations are perfect for a relaxing getaway for anyone.
- **Chelsea Pines** (3, B3; ☎ 212-929-1023; www.chelseapinesinn.com; 317 W 14th St btwn Eighth & Ninth Aves; mid-range; A, C, E to 14th St, L to Eighth Ave) It's gay-man central at this sweet, unique little inn. Rooms are small but homey.
- **Colonial House Inn** (3, B3; ☎ 212-243-9669; www.colonialhouseinn.com; 318 W 22nd St btwn Eighth & Ninth Aves; budget–mid-range; C, E to 23rd St) Serene and graceful, but with upbeat charm, this B&B has a rooftop deck for nude sunbathers.
- **Incentra Village House** (3, B4; ☎ 212-206-0007; 32 Eighth Ave at 12th St; mid-range; A, C, E to 14th St) Built in 1841, these two landmark townhouses were the city's first gay inn. The 12 rooms get booked way in advance.

About New York City

HISTORY

Long before Giovanni da Verrazano sailed by Staten Island in 1524, or Henry Hudson came looking for land to claim for the Dutch East India Company in 1609, great numbers of Algonquin-speaking people had made the Manhattan area their home.

An Island of Hills

The Lenape Natives fished New York Bay for oysters and striped bass, and laid down well worn trading routes across the hilly island (Manhattan means 'island of hills' in one native dialect); those same routes later became Broadway, Amsterdam Ave and other large city thoroughfares. Legend says that Dutch trader Peter Minuit bought the island from the Lenape for trinkets worth about $24, but historians say it's unlikely the Lenape agreed to anything of the sort, since it was a culture that didn't adhere to the idea of private property. In any case, the Dutch assumed control of the island and by 1630 the colony numbered 270, with a number of Belgians (Walloons), French Huguenots and English mixed in.

Colonial Era

Peter Stuyvesant arrived to impose order on the unruly colony of New Amsterdam in 1647, but his intolerant religious views led to unrest. Few resisted the bloodless coup by the British in 1664, and the colony was renamed as New York. It be-

Ellis Island: first port of call for millions

came a British stronghold and remained steadfastly loyal to George III through much of the Revolutionary War in the 1770s. George Washington's ragtag army of farm boys was almost wiped out by Britain's General Cornwallis and his troops in what is currently Brooklyn Heights – only a daring, all-night march north saved them.

Boom Years

Post-Revolutionary times were good for most New Yorkers, even though the founding fathers disliked the bustling seaport city. The capital moved further south but the masses didn't go with it, and by 1830 the population had expanded to 250,000, mostly composed of immigrants working in dangerous factories and living in tenements on the Lower East Side. At the same time, corrupt politicians bilked millions from public works projects and industrial barons amassed tax-free fortunes. A lack of space forced building sprawl upward rather than outward; skyscrapers peppered the horizon and the city continued to expand its network of subways and elevated trains. In 1898 the independent districts of Staten Island, Queens, the Bronx and Brooklyn merged with Manhattan into the five 'boroughs' of New York City. With wave after wave of immigrants arriving, the population reached three million in 1900.

The Jazz Age and beyond

Speakeasies, flappers, gangsters, the 19th Amendment (which gave women the right to vote) and a Harlem Renaissance brought incredible vitality to New York in the years preceding and following WWI. Margaret Sanger preached about birth control in Washington Sq Park, Wall St made golden boys out of hayseeds, and F Scott Fitzgerald chronicled it all in *The Great Gatsby*. When the bottom fell out of the stock market on Black Tuesday (October 29, 1929) the glittering, apparently limitless future of New York was smashed overnight. Hard times followed and, even though Manhattan was the nation's premier city after WWII, economically things continued to stagnate. Only a massive federal loan program rescued the city from bankruptcy in the 1970s.

> ### African Burial Ground
> Africans have been in New York City since the 17th-century Dutch era. Brought over as slaves, they built many of the colonial attractions of Lower Manhattan. Their contributions were largely forgotten as slavery disappeared from the north, but the African Burial Ground – the final resting place of some 400 slaves taken mostly from Ghana that was discovered accidentally in 1991 – is a poignant reminder. The site is at Duane and Broadway, and a permanent exhibition is on display at the Schomberg Center in Harlem (p27).

Modern Times

Republican Rudolph Giuliani was elected mayor in 1992 and immediately instituted a series of 'Quality of Life' initiatives, which involved intense police crackdowns on crime and seedy areas like Times Sq (now scrubbed clean). It was very successful at first but, as more people moved to the city, rents skyrocketed, long-time residents were pushed out and roiling class and racial tensions surfaced, made worse when police mistook a wallet for a gun and shot 41 bullets at an unarmed African immigrant in February 1998 – mortally striking him 19 times. Thousands took to the streets in protest. But on September 11, 2001, it was Giuliani who allayed New Yorker's fears in the face of terrorism. His leadership restored the city's faith, but term limits made it impossible to reelect him. The leadership role went to billionaire businessman Michael Bloomberg, whose steady (but unimpassioned) style got the city back on track. Some of his decisions have been wildly unpopular (refusing to let protestors rally in Central Park, for example, when the Republican National Convention came in August 2004), but he's also widely

A 'Quality of Life' initiative: cops at Times Sq

applauded for his moderate stance on most issues and relatively pro-environment views. New development projects are breathing fresh life into parts of Brooklyn (a stadium is being built to house its new basketball team), and a huge sports complex is in the works for the Upper West Side – both are part of an ambitious plan to land the Olympic Games for New York City in 2012.

ENVIRONMENT

Most New Yorkers are die-hard recycling enthusiasts (although you'll be hard-pressed to find any recycling receptacles on the streets) and have a reverence for the green spaces poking through the concrete jungle. They've also clamored for a cleanup of the Hudson River (contaminated with a toxic sludge of dangerous chemicals in the north) and, thanks to the constant pressure, much progress has been made. New Yorkers now enjoy the river like never before, aided by the five miles of bike and pedestrian paths of Hudson River Park. The big battle these days is the Croton Watershed upstate, which supplies the city with its abundant supply of drinking water. New Yorkers

Christopher St pier: green-friendly

say 'hands off' but real estate developers aren't letting go of what they see as a prime chunk of land. It's a détente for the moment, but a big Bronx-style showdown may be in the offing.

GOVERNMENT & POLITICS

New York City is as Democratic as they come, although a few Republicans have ascended to high posts. Although far from perfect, the social benefits offered by the city are much better than any found in neighboring states; people have moved to New York just to access the public assistance programs. That said, a great number of working New Yorkers live paycheck to paycheck; the influx of undocumented immigrants creates a labor force ripe for exploitation and constant rent hikes can force families to turn over almost all their monthly earnings to a landlord. Others, of course, live a very different reality, earning big bucks in high finance and film, fashion and retail industries. Affordable housing, the environment and the protection of constitutional and civil rights are big issues for New Yorkers. The city has five borough presidents, a city-wide comptroller, a public advocate and a 51-member city council to balance the mayoral power, but when New Yorkers really have something to say, they take to the streets and do it themselves.

ECONOMY

New York City's economic star was on the wane in early 2000, as the nation entered its first economic slump in eight years. The downward slide gained rapid momentum in the wake of 9/11, and it took two years before the city started to get some pep in its financial step again. The economy has yet to return to the record highs of the late 1990s, but the city's general prosperity is apparent in its bustling shops, busy restaurants and crowded Broadway shows. Most importantly, New York still pulls in the tourists, which adds $40 million to the city coffers annually. That, along with tax revenue from the many major corporations (foreign and domestic) headquartered here, looks set to keep the city firmly in the black for the immediate future.

> ### Did You Know?
> - There are 226 miles of subway in New York City
> - There are 6,375 miles of streets in New York City
> - The world's largest Halloween Parade takes place annually in Greenwich Village on October 31
> - As late as the 1840s, thousands of pigs roamed Wall Street to consume garbage – an early sanitation system
> - Author Jack London once lived as a hobo in City Hall Park
> - The *Titanic* was scheduled to dock at Chelsea Piers on completion of her maiden voyage
> - The New York Yankees baseball team has won the World Series 26 times

SOCIETY & CULTURE

New York City is the original 'melting pot,' the term used by the nation's leaders to encourage mixing between old settlers and new arrivals at the turn of the 20th century. Popular theory held that incoming immigrants would assimilate to the dominant culture (which was primarily Anglo-Saxon at the time) and create a unified population free of ethnic and class divisions. Instead the opposite happened: Italians coming into New York City didn't settle in the Irish enclave of Greenwich Village, or the Eastern European Jewish communities of the Lower East Side. They established their own beachhead which became known as Little Italy and proudly spoke their language and practiced their traditions. Dominicans of the 1950s and 1960s settled in what became Spanish Harlem, and Puerto Ricans still own most of the Bronx. Along the way other nationalities arrived and rubbed shoulders and traded quips, and if the perfect homogeneity the city planners envisioned never materialized, well, nobody misses it because a vibrant hybrid culture of multi-culti influences has taken its place. No matter what their ethnic roots, your average New Yorker today knows a smattering of Spanish or another foreign language (or is perfectly bilingual), has a good sense of the Chinese lunar calendar (how else to know when the Chinese New Year is coming with its fabulous dragon parade?) and can order a bagel with a *schmear* (dab of cream cheese) without batting an eyelid.

Which is not to say that all New Yorkers live together in perfect harmony – in a city of more than 8 million, there are bound to be a few problems. Politicians are expected to resolve most of these conflicts and if they don't, they can kiss that second term goodbye. When it comes to the city's overall well-being, New Yorkers have no problem banding together in amazing displays of solidarity.

The original 'melting pot'

Dos and Don'ts

Something has happened to New Yorkers in recent years – they've gotten friendlier. Everything is still done double-time, but exchanging one-liners while on the fly is a highly prized skill. You'll hear such exchanges everywhere ('How you doin', Hey, what's happening, You got the time, buddy?') so don't hold back if someone sends a well meaning inquiry your way. Politeness – please, thank you, etc – is also important, and displays of class status like slighting the taxi driver or doorman do not go over well in democratic New York. There are a few things that raise local ire: do not exit the subway stairs and stop to pull out your map, thereby blocking the exit. Move to the corner and then look. Don't go into an eatery during the busy lunch hour rush and keep everyone waiting while you decide. You're just asking for the counterperson to zing you with a typical New York barb. Hang back until you are ready to order. A jacket and tie are expected at upscale restaurants, but otherwise feel free to wear what you wish.

Smoke Rings

The non-smoking law of 2002 has created a rash of speakeasy-type establishments where the impure can still puff. Since smoking is prohibited in restaurants, cafés, public spaces and buildings, you have to look for restaurants and bars with outdoor cafés if you want to smoke, or be prepared to step outside. The East Village is your best bet if you want a restaurant that's flouting authority.

ARTS

Don't let New York's staunchly capitalist demeanor fool you into thinking that only the art of the deal matters here; creative expression hums on even the most humble street corner. On any given night the city's numerous theaters, shows and dance halls are packed full.

Dance

New York is home to an amazing assortment of prominent dance companies and choreographers such as Martha Graham, the New York City Ballet and the Alvin Ailey Dance Troupe. It also nurtures the talented Ballet Folklorico Mexicano, Chen & Dancers and the Repetorio Español, three highly acclaimed companies devoted to traditional and ethnic dance.

Film

The annual Tribeca Film Festival brings Hollywood types and cineasts to Manhattan in droves, but new art-house features, indie premieres and alternative film festivals are on all the time. There's a Latin Film Festival, an Italian Film Festival, festivals dedicated to shorts, animation, documentaries and more. High profile directors like Sofia Coppola, Spike Lee and Martin Scorsese help keep the city in the camera's eye; it's featured in some 200 films a year.

Literature

Perhaps no other city in America has had such a profound impact on the nation's literary canon. From Walt Whitman's evocative odes to Jay McInerney's *Bright Lights, Big City*, New York has inspired countless artists to put pen to paper. Jonathan Franzen, author of *The Corrections*, wrote many of his first works from a small studio in northern Manhattan; Colin Whitehead, author of *The Institutionalist*, writes with one eye on the city skyline for inspiration. Spoken word events are alive and well, particularly in Harlem and the East Village/Lower East Side. Readings from new authors are held often at area bookstores.

Music

The Big Apple has always had great blues and jazz, but it was the infamous art/punk scene of the 1960s and '70s that really revitalized the city's musical energy during economic bad times. Born on the Bowery, the punk scene met and intertwined (in interesting and sometimes startling ways) with the folk scene at the Chelsea Hotel, embodied perhaps by the eclectic crossover appeal of Janis Joplin and Jimi Hendrix. Hard rock and indie music continue to hold court on the Lower East Side with the occasional foray into Midtown.

How do you get to Carnegie Hall? Practice, practice, practice. If you want to attend a concert there rather than give one, you'll find it much easier to get in. Irving Berlin, Gustav Mahler, Leonard Bernstein, Arturo Toscanini all did it the hard way. Hip hop and rap stars, long marginalized on the edges of mainstream music, broke through by packing clubs in Midtown and Harlem for live performances.

The latest generation of jazz artists, lead by Wynton and Branford Marsalis, play big venues like Carnegie Hall and the new Jazz Center at Time Warner, but also regularly drop by more intimate clubs.

Hey, don't turn your back on the Ramones!

Painting

The city is synonymous with certain artists and movements: Pop Art, Abstract Expressionism, Street Art, Andy Warhol, Jackson Pollack and Jean-Michel Basquiat. The underground art culture created by Warhol in the 1960s lives on in the work shown in Chelsea galleries, although the artists themselves often live in Brooklyn or beyond.

Photography

You can hardly turn around in Manhattan without bumping into someone's zoom lens. Herb Ritts, Richard Avedon and Annie Liebowitz all keep or kept studios here. Major retrospectives of artists like Lotte Jacobi or Man Ray are frequent, and esteemed photog Graham Nash can often be seen stalking the perfect shot on city streets.

Theater

Now that Broadway has rediscovered big musical shows, edgier and more thoughtful pieces go 'off-Broadway,' meaning smaller venues in the West or East Village. 'Off-off Broadway' is reserved for very fringe or experimental pieces in tiny places around the Bowery. That doesn't mean they aren't good: many win national awards and go on to be produced in larger spaces. For works from modern playwrights like Wendy Wasserman or Suzann-Lori Parks, stay below 23rd St, but for a Rodgers & Hammerstein extravaganza, you know it's got to be 42nd St.

The Return of the Chocolate Smeared Woman

Karen Finley, a renowned performance artist, ran afoul of one US Senator when she won a grant from the National Endowment of the Arts for a piece that involved smearing herself with chocolate sauce while naked. The Senator demanded 'decency standards' be followed when awarding grants, igniting cries of censorship from artists. Finley took her case to the courts and lost, but did get the last laugh. Backed by an enthusiastic public she staged a comeback show a year later: The Return of the Chocolate Smeared Woman. She is a frequent performer in the East Village.

Directory

'We'll huff and we'll puff and we'll blow this shop down' – the Meatpacking District

ARRIVAL & DEPARTURE
Air

New York is connected to just about every major city in North America and Western Europe via direct flights. As a general rule most domestic flights come into LaGuardia Airport (6, B1), international flights are served by John F Kennedy Airport (4, C2) and both domestic and international flights arrive in Newark Liberty Airport (4, A3) in New Jersey. New York City's two airports lie about 30 minutes east of the city but traffic often turns that into a two-hour drive, so many people prefer to head to Newark, which is more easily accessed via public transportation and highway. For information on getting to the three airports, call the **Air Ride Line** (☎ 800-247-7433; www.panynj.gov/aviation/avmain; ☺ 8am-6pm Mon-Fri).

JFK INTERNATIONAL AIRPORT

John F Kennedy International Airport (4, C2), in southeastern Queens, is about 15 miles (24km) from Midtown, or 45 to 75 minutes by car – longer in peak hours.

Left Luggage

Facilities at Terminals 1 and 4 charge approximately $9 per bag.

Information

General inquiries	☎ 718-244-4444
Parking information	☎ 718-244-4444
Hotel booking service	☎ 212-267-5500

Airport Access

Subway/Air Train The subway ride to Howard Beach–JFK Station takes around one hour from Midtown. Take the A train marked Far Rockaway or Rockaway Park. Disembark at Howard Beach, then switch to the Air Train ($5 one-way, plus subway fare), which runs every four to eight minutes from 6am to 11pm. This will take you to any of the terminals, the airport parking lot and even to some of the nearby car rental agencies. The E, J and Z subway and the Long Island Rail Road to Jamaica, Queens also links to the Air Train.

Bus The **New York Airport Service** (☎ 718-875-8200) buses run every 15 to 20 minutes from 5am to midnight. They stop at Penn Station (3, B2), Port Authority Bus Terminal (2, B9) and Grand Central Station (2, D8). Allow 60 to 75 minutes for the trip ($13 one way).

Taxi The fare to Manhattan is a flat $45 plus tolls and tip. This flat rate is only available from the airport.

Shared Ride Expect to pay about $15 per person; call **SuperShuttle** (☎ 212-258-3826; www.super shuttle.net).

Car Service This costs around $50. Operators include **Big Apple** (☎ 718-232-1015), **Citywide** (☎ 718-405-5822) or **Dial** (☎ 718-743-2877).

LAGUARDIA AIRPORT

LaGuardia (6, B1) is in northern Queens, 8 miles (13km) from Midtown, or 20 to 45 minutes by car.

Left Luggage

There are no left-luggage facilities.

Information

General inquiries	☎ 718-533-3400
Parking information	☎ 718-533-3400
Hotel booking service	☎ 212-267-5500

Airport Access

Bus From the airport, take the M60 to W 106th St and Broadway. The M60 also connects with the N and W trains in Astoria Queens, the 4, 5, 6, 2, 3, A, B, C, D subways along 125th St and the 1, 9 subway at 116th, 110th Sts and Broadway.

Alternatively, use the **New York Airport Service** (☎ 718-875-8200; www.nyairportservice.com). Buses leave every 20 minutes between 6am and midnight from Penn Station (3, B2), the Port Authority Bus Terminal (2, B9) and Grand Central Station (2, D8). The ride costs $12 and takes about 30 minutes.

Taxi The fare is around $25 to $40 plus tolls and tips.

Shared Ride This will cost about $14 per person; call **SuperShuttle** (see p000).

Car Service Expect to pay around $40 plus tolls and tips. Contact the companies listed on p000.

NEWARK LIBERTY INTERNATIONAL AIRPORT

Situated in New Jersey, about 15 miles (19km) west of Manhattan, Newark (4, A3) is a 30 to 60 minute drive from the city.

Left Luggage

There are no left-luggage facilities.

Information

General inquiries ☎ 973-961-6000
Parking information ☎ 973-961-6000
Hotel booking service ☎ 212-267-5500

Airport Access

There are a number of ways to get out to Newark, New Jersey. (Note: the train station in Newark is also called Penn Station – don't confuse it with New York's Penn Station; they are two different entities.)

Train Take NJ Transit from New York's Penn Station to Newark Liberty International Airport Station ($11.55 one way). Alternatively, take the NJ PATH train ($2) to Newark Penn Station and connect to the NJ Transit train to the airport ($6.80). Once at the airport you will have to get on the Air Train (free with NJ Transit ticket) to get to your terminal or parking lot. NJ PATH stations can be found at Christopher St, 14th St, 23rd St, and 33rd St near Herald Sq. The World Trade Center PATH is also operational again. Take the train labeled 'NWK' for Newark.

Bus Take **Olympia Airport Express** (☎ 212-964-6233, 908-354-3330) from the Port Authority Bus Terminal (2, B9), New York's Penn Station (3, B2), Grand Central Terminal (2, D8) or the World Trade Center (3, C7); the fare is $12. For a cheaper option ($4), take bus No 107, which has numerous stops on the way to the airport.

Taxi The fare costs about $50 plus $10 for tolls and extra for tips.

Port Authority Ferry It's possible to take a ferry from New York across the Hudson River to New Jersey and pick up a PATH train there ($6; www.panynj.gov/ferry/fermain.HTM). The ferry ride is a scenic, albeit short (10 minutes), part of the journey; however, the Hoboken stop is the only one that deposits you right near a PATH station. Colgate and other stops require a few minutes walk to get on the PATH. Not a good idea for those with heavy luggage.

Shared Ride Expect to pay around $20 per person; call **SuperShuttle** (see p000).

Car Service Fees start around $60. See the companies listed on p000.

Bus

Out-of-state buses arrive at and depart from **Port Authority Bus Terminal** (2, B9; ☎ 212-564-8484; 625 Eighth Ave) with carriers going to just about anywhere in the US and parts of Canada. An inexpensive bus route that has opened up recently is the 'Chinatown to Chinatown' line. Run by **Fung-Wah Company** (☎ 212-925-8889; www.fungwahbus.com), the bus leaves out of New York's Chinatown and goes directly to the Chinatowns in

Boston or Washington, DC; the fare is $15 one way.

Train

Long-distance Amtrak trains arrive at **Pennsylvania (Penn) Station** (3, B2; ☎ 212-582-6875, 800-872-7245; 33rd St btwn Seventh & Eighth Aves). Commuter trains (MetroNorth) use **Grand Central Terminal** (2, D8; ☎ 212-532-4900; Park Ave at 42nd St). **New Jersey PATH** (Port Authority Trans-Hudson; ☎ 800-234-7284) trains stop at several stations in Manhattan but don't venture above 33rd St.

Travel Documents

PASSPORT

Visitors are now required to have a passport that's valid for at least six months after their intended stay in the USA.

VISA

According to the US State Department, many Canadian citizens and many citizens from Visa Waiver Program countries can come to the US without a visa if they meet certain requirements. To find out what those requirements are, check with the American embassy nearest you. Most of Western Europe participates in the Visa Waiver Program, so residents of the UK, Ireland, Norway, Spain, France, Germany, and also Australia and New Zealand usually do not need visas for temporary visits (but must carry a valid passport that can be scanned). Visitors from other countries will need to apply for a visa at the nearest American embassy, and allow at least six weeks for the paperwork to go through. Many of the application forms and further information can be found at the US State Department website (http://travel.state.gov/visa).

RETURN/ONWARD TICKET

To enter, you need a return ticket that's nonrefundable in the USA.

Customs & Duty Free

If you are carrying more than $10,000 in US and/or foreign cash, traveler's checks or money orders when you enter the USA, you must declare it. You can import 1L of liquor (if you are over the age of 21); 200 cigarettes, 50 cigars (provided they are not Cuban) or 2kg of tobacco; and gifts up to a total value of $100 ($400 for US citizens).

Security

Expect security to be very visible and tight. Cars are not allowed to linger for longer than a few seconds at any airport, so be ready to hop out quickly at your terminal. Allow extra time for check-in and always have your identification on hand. Sky cab or curbside luggage check-in is now mostly prohibited. The following items cannot be brought onto airplanes either on your person or in your carry-on luggage at any of New York City's three airports:

Knives Any cutting and puncturing instruments such as Swiss Army knives, pocketknives, box cutters, ice picks, straight razors, scissors, and metal nail files.

Athletic equipment Anything that could be used as a weapon, such as baseball/softball bats, golf clubs, pool cues, ski poles and hockey sticks.

Weapons Firearms, ammunition, gunpowder, mace, tear gas or pepper spray.

Aerosol spray cans Hairspray, deodorant, insect repellant or butane fuel (such as in curling iron refills, scuba tanks, propane tanks, cartridges and self-inflating rafts).

Explosives Fireworks, sparklers or signal flares.

Flammable liquids or solids Fuel, paints, paint thinners or cleaners, lighter fluid and perfume (no more than 16 oz).

Other hazardous or dangerous items Corkscrews, blades of any type or size, dry ice, gas-powered tools, wet-cell batteries, camping equipment with fuel, radioactive materials, poisons, infectious substances.

GETTING AROUND

Manhattan's grid system gets packed with traffic during the daytime rush hours (a phenomenon known as 'gridlock'). The subway is generally the fastest, cheapest way to get around. City buses can be useful if you are traveling north–south, provided that traffic is moving. Pick up a public transit map from subway ticket booths. Taxis are the most convenient mode of transportation after 1am.

Travel Passes

MetroCard (☎ 718-330-1234) is the easiest way to pay for travel on New York's public transit system. Pick one up at any newsstand or subway booth. The one-day Fun Pass is a major money saver, giving you unlimited access to subways and buses from the first swipe until 3am the next morning. For longer stays grab a seven-day or 30-day unlimited card. Pay-per-ride options are also available – a subway clerk will put any dollar amount you want on your MetroCard, with bonus rides when you buy several at a time. Be aware that the single-ride cards sold from machines in subway stations expire after two hours. At print time, the single ride fare was $2, though that's subject to change.

Subway

The subway system (☎ 718-330-1234) runs 24 hours per day. It's an occasionally humid and smelly network, but it gets the job done. In this book, our subway listings note the nearest stop's name.

Bus

City buses (☎ 718-330-1234) operate 24 hours per day and generally run north–south along avenues and crosstown along the major east–west thoroughfares. You need exact change of $2 or a MetroCard to board a bus.

Bus routes that begin and end in Manhattan start with M (eg M5); Queens bus routes start with Q, Brooklyn with B, and the Bronx with BX. Some 'Limited Stop' buses pull over only every 10 blocks or so, but at night you can ask to be let off at any point along the route. 'Express' buses ($6.50) are primarily for outer-borough commuters, not for people taking short trips.

Train

New Jersey PATH trains (☎ 800-234-7284) run down Sixth Ave to Jersey City, Hoboken and Newark, with stops at 33rd, 23rd, 14th, 9th and Christopher Sts in Manhattan. A second line goes from the World Trade Center to Jersey City and Newark. These reliable trains run every 15 to 45 minutes 24 hours a day. The fare is currently $1.50.

Boat

New York Waterway (☎ 800-533-3779) ferries make runs up the Hudson River Valley and from Midtown to Yankee Stadium (4, B1) in the Bronx. A popular commuter route goes from the New Jersey Transit train station in Hoboken (4, A2) to the World Financial Center in Lower Manhattan (3, C8); boats leave every five to 10 minutes at peak times, and the 10 minute ride costs $4 each way.

Port Authority Ferries (www.panynj.gov/ferry/fermain.HTM) run between Battery Park and New Jersey, stopping mainly at Hoboken and Colgate (Exchange Place), across from Lower Manhattan.

New York Water Taxi (☎ 212-742-1969; www.nywatertaxi.com;

one-stop $5) is a new service that's really taken off in New York. These yellow taxi boats stop at various piers along Manhattan's West Side and are a wonderful way to travel to Midtown, lower Manhattan, and even parts of Brooklyn and Queens.

Taxi

Taxis are available when the rooftop license number is lit (as opposed to the 'off duty' side lights). Fares are metered and start at $2.50; tip is 10% to 15% (minimum 50¢). There's a 50¢ surcharge from 8pm to 6am. For long trips uptown or downtown, ask the driver to take the FDR Highway (East Side) or West Side Highway (West Side).

Limousine

Limousines and car services can be an inexpensive way to travel, especially for groups. **Affordable Limousine Service** (☎ 888-338-4567) and **Carmel** (☎ 212-666-6666) charge about $45 per hour for up to four people; a night on the town (ie three hours) for eight costs $150.

Car & Motorcycle

Try to avoid renting or driving a motor vehicle into New York if possible. Parking is a nightmare, traffic can steal hours from your day, and the cost of gasoline keeps creeping ever upward. Any convenience it might momentarily afford will be lost when you circle that block for the umpteenth time waiting for a spot to open up, or pull into a parking garage and fork over $25 for the first hour. Motorcycles are marginally easier to squeeze into spaces, but it's really not worth the hassle when cabs and subways are so readily available.

RENTAL

Car rental is expensive, and cheaper airport deals are rare. Organise a package deal before you arrive.

The main rental agencies in New York City include **Avis** (☎ 800-331-1212), **Budget** (☎ 800-527-0700), **Dollar** (☎ 800-800-4000), **Hertz** (☎ 800-654-3131) and **Thrifty** (☎ 800-367-2277).

ROAD RULES

Drive on the right-hand side of the road, and don't block intersections – the wrath of other drivers is worse than the stiff penalties you may incur. All front seat occupants must wear seat belts; all back seat occupants under the age of 10 must wear seatbelts or another suitable restraint.

Driving with a blood alcohol level of .05 (.02 if you're under 21) or above is against the law. The state maximum speed limit is 55mph (just over 70km/h); however, watch for lower limits on city streets and in school zones.

DRIVER'S LICENSE

If you intend to drive, you will need a license from your home country, showing your address, full name and country of origin.

MOTORING ORGANIZATIONS

The **American Automobile Association** (AAA; ☎ 212-757-2000) is a national auto club that offers directions, maps and emergency road service (☎ 800-AAA-HELP), plus travel agent assistance. You may want to join if you'll be driving a lot and membership could entitle you to reduced hotel rates.

PRACTICALITIES
Business Hours

Office hours are Monday to Friday 9am to 5pm. Most shops are open Monday to Saturday 10am to 6pm and Sunday noon to 6pm, with some extended hours Thursday nights; some bakeries and clothing shops close Monday. Some businesses change their operating hours with the seasons, usually resulting in shorter hours in winter months. A few places do the opposite, preferring to have weekends off and to work shorter days in the summer.

Museums and art galleries are usually open Tuesday to Sunday 10am to 5pm. On public holidays, banks, schools and government offices (including post offices) close, and transportation services operate on a Sunday schedule.

Climate & When to Go

There are always lots of tourists in New York City, although numbers decline slightly in January and February. The most pleasant and temperate times to visit are May, early June and mid-September to October (but hotel prices can be high). Wet weather is common in November and April. Snow typically falls from December to February, although a late-March nor'easter always pops up. High average temperatures and humidity, together with poor air quality, can make for an uncomfortable summer.

NEW YORK, NY 39m (131ft)

Disabled Travelers

Federal laws require that all government offices have good elevator and ramp access for wheelchairs and devices to aid the hearing impaired. Almost all major venues offer good bathroom facilities for those with wheelchairs, and all city buses are able to carry wheelchair passengers. Only some subway stations are accessible (see MTA maps or call ☎ 718-596-8585).

Listings in this book that are wheelchair-friendly are indicated by the ♿ icon and rated from 'limited' to 'excellent'. 'Limited' denotes a minimal level of accessibility, while 'excellent' applies to places that offer full access to all sights and attractions.

Information & Organizations

The book *Access for All* is a disabled guide to New York attractions. Contact **Hospital Audiences** (☎ 212-575-7676; www.hospital audiences.org; 548 Broadway, New York, NY 10012) for a copy.

Helpful contacts include:

New York Society for the Deaf (☎ 212-777-3900)

People with Disabilities Office (☎ 212-788-2830, TTY 212-788-2838)

Public Transport Accessible Line (☎ 718-596-8585, TTY 800-734-7433)

Society for Accessible Travel and Hospitality (SATH; ☎ 212-447-7284; www.sath.org)

Discounts

Students, children (under 12) and seniors get discounts at most attractions and on most forms of transportation. Many attractions also offer reduced-price tickets for families. Students must present university IDs for discounts. Seniors over 62 can also expect cut rates on hotel charges, drugstore (pharmacy) prescriptions and cinema prices. Buy a CityPass (www .citypass.com) to avoid long ticket lines at six major attractions and for a 50% discount on admission.

Electricity

Electricity in the USA is 110V and 60Hz. Plugs have two or three pins (two flat pins, often with a round 'grounding' pin). Adapters for European and South American plugs are widely available; Australians should bring adapters.

Embassies & Consulates

The UN's presence in New York means that nearly every country in the world maintains diplomatic offices here. Most are listed in the white pages of the phone book under 'Consulates General of (country).' Some embassies include:

Australia (2, 07; ☎ 212-351-6500; 150 E 42nd St btwn Lexington & Third Aves)

Canada (2, M5; ☎ 212-596-1783; 1251 Sixth Ave btwn 49th & 50th Sts)

Ireland (2, M7; ☎ 212-319-2555; 345 Park Ave btwn 51st & 52nd Sts)

New Zealand (2, M7; ☎ 212-832-4038; 780 Third Ave btwn 48th & 49th Sts)

South Africa (2, 08; ☎ 212-213-4880; 333 E 38th St btwn First & Second Aves)

UK (2, M7; ☎ 212-745-0202; 845 Third Ave btwn 51st & 52nd Sts)

Emergencies

Although Manhattan has a reputation as a big, bad city, the last serious crime wave was in the 1970s. Violent crimes are at their lowest ever, with streets populated at all hours. It's always better to take a cab late at night, but mostly the city's safe to traverse on foot well past midnight (one caveat: don't go deep into Central Park on your own or in a small group past 11pm).

Police, fire, ambulance (☎ 911)

Police information operator (☎ 212-374-5000)

Fitness

You can keep yourself in fighting form by picking up a day pass for about US$20 from almost any local gym. Ask at your front desk; hotels without their own gyms often have arrangements with area facilities that allow guests special privileges.

Chelsea Piers (3, A3; ☎ 212-336-6000; www.chelseapiers.com; 23rd St at Hudson River) has a thousand ways to make you sweat. Choose from skating, horseback riding, indoor rockwall climbing, indoor golf and bowling.

BASKETBALL

A pick-up game is always on somewhere, but you'd better come prepared with an A game. Check out the courts at W 4th St & Sixth Ave (3, C4) for high-quality hoops.

RUNNING

Manhattan has some great traffic-free spots. For starters, there's Central Park's 6.2 mile roadway, which loops around the park. This is closed to cars from 7pm Friday to 6am Monday year-round. From January to late November, it's also closed from 10am to 3pm and 7pm to 10pm Monday to Friday. Other spots include the soft 1 mile path that encircles the Jacqueline Kennedy Onassis Reservoir; the Hudson River path (Battery Park to 125th St) and an esplanade along the East River. The **New York Road Runners Club** (☎ 212-860-4455) organizes regular runs in the city.

SKATING

Show off your inline skating skills (or lack thereof) at Central Park, on the mall that runs east of the Sheep Meadow. If you're just starting out, rent a pair from the nearby **Blades West** (2, B5; ☎ 212-787-3911; 120 W 72nd St) and ask a volunteer at the W 72nd St entrance to show you how to stop.

The Chelsea Piers complex has roller rinks and ramps, and the path along the Hudson between Battery Park and 125th St goes right by here.

SWIMMING

In summer 50 city pools open for free. Some pools set aside lap swimming times; the rest of the time they tend to be taken over by dive-bombing kids. For a list of pools, check out the **Parks Department** website (www.nycgovparks.org).

Gay & Lesbian Travelers

New York is one of the most gay-friendly cities on earth, and several neighborhoods – particularly Greenwich Village and Chelsea in Manhattan, Jackson Heights in Queens and Park Slope in Brooklyn – are populated by many gays and lesbians. The age of consent for homosexual sex is 17 (the same as for heterosexual sex). Clubs, hotels and restaurants often indicate they are 'gay-friendly' by displaying a rainbow flag, but that speaks more to the establishment's sensibilities than a policy. In fact, there are very few places in New York that aren't populated with a mixed crowd on any given night.

INFORMATION & ORGANIZATIONS

The free magazines *HX* and *Next* are available at restaurants and bars. Look for *LGNY* and *NY Blade* in street-corner boxes. Pick up the lifestyle magazine *Metrosource* at shops and the Lesbian & Gay Community Services Center. *Time Out* features a good events section.

Useful counseling, referral and information centers include:

Gay & Lesbian Hotline (☎ 212-989-0999; glnh@glnh.org)

Lesbian & Gay Community Services Center (☎ 212-620-7310; www.gaycenter.org; 208 W 13th St at Seventh Ave)

Health
IMMUNIZATIONS

No immunizations are required to enter the US.

PRECAUTIONS

New York tap water is safe to drink; even so, many residents drink bottled or filtered water. Encephalitis outbreaks sometimes prompt citywide spraying and advice that residents should wear long sleeves and mosquito repellent, but generally New York is as healthy as other big, dirty cities.

Practice the usual precautions when it comes to sex; condoms are available from drugstores and nightclub vending machines.

MEDICAL SERVICES

Travel insurance is advised to cover any medical treatment. **New York Hotel Urgent Medical Services** (☎ 212-737-1212) offers medical services to visitors; doctors make 24-hour house (and hotel) calls. Prices start at $200, including most medication.

All hospitals have 24-hour emergency departments.

Bellevue Hospital (3, E2; ☎ 212-562-4141; NYU Medical Center, First Ave at E 27th St)

Lenox Hill Hospital (2, D5; ☎ 212-434-2000; 100 E 77th St btwn Park & Lexington Aves)

New York Hospital (2, E6; ☎ 212-746-5050; 525 E 68th St btwn York Ave & Franklin D Roosevelt Dr)

DENTAL SERVICES

If you chip a tooth or require emergency treatment, head to the **Stuyvesant Dentist Association** (3, E3; ☎ 212-473-4151; 430 E 20th St at First Ave).

PHARMACIES

There are a number of 24-hour pharmacies in New York City:

Duane Reade (2, C7; ☎ 212-541-9708; W 57th St at Broadway)

Duane Reade (3, C4; ☎ 212-674-5357; Sixth Ave at Waverly Pl)

Genovese (2, E6; ☎ 212-772-0104; 1299 Second Ave at 68th St)

Holidays
New Year's Day January 1
Martin Luther King Jr Day 3rd Monday in January

Presidents' Day 3rd Monday in February
Easter Sunday March/April
Memorial Day Last Monday in May
Independence Day July 4
Labor Day 1st Monday in September
Columbus Day 2nd Monday in October
Veterans' Day November 11
Thanksgiving Day 4th Thursday in November
Christmas Day December 25

Imperial System

Americans hate the metric system and continue to resist it. Distances are in feet, yards and miles. Dry weights are measured by the ounce, pound and ton; liquid measures differ from dry measures. Gasoline is dispensed by the US gallon (about 20% less than the imperial gallon). US pints and quarts are also 20% less than imperial ones.

TEMPERATURE
$°C = (°F - 32) \div 1.8$
$°F = (°C \times 1.8) + 32$

DISTANCE
1in = 2.54cm
1cm = 0.39in
1m = 3.3ft = 1.1yd
1ft = 0.3m
1km = 0.62 miles
1 mile = 1.6km

WEIGHT
1kg = 2.2lb
1lb = 0.45kg
1g = 0.04oz
1oz = 28g

VOLUME
1L = 0.26 US gallons
1 US gallon = 3.8L
1L = 0.22 imperial gallons
1 imperial gallon = 4.55L

Internet

Public libraries offer free web access; Internet cafés are common.

INTERNET SERVICE PROVIDERS

Major national ISPs include **AOL** (dial-in: ☎ 212-871-1021) and **AT&T** (dial-in: ☎ 212-824-2405).

Earthlink (www.earthlink.net) is another popular ISP while **Metconnect** (☎ 212-359-2000, 646-496-0000; www.metconnect.com) offers a free service.

INTERNET CAFÉS

EasyEverything (2, C8; ☎ 212-398-0775; www.easyeverything.com; W 42nd St btwn Seventh & Eighth Aves; prices vary; 🕑 24hr)
NY Computer Café (2, E7; ☎ 212-872-1704; www.nycomputercafe.com; 274 E 57th St btwn Second & Third Aves; per hr $12; 🕑 8am-11pm Mon-Fri, 10am-11pm Sat, 11am-11pm Sun)
Times Sq Cybercafe (2, C8; ☎ 212-333-4109; www.cyber-cafe.com; 250 W 49th St btwn Broadway & Eighth Ave; per 1/2 hr $6.40; 🕑 8am-11pm Mon-Fri, 11am-11pm Sat-Sun)

WIFI

Bryant Park has a wireless network that works with any laptop or handheld device with an 802.11b compatible wireless card or built-in 802.11b wireless capability. Instructions on how to configure your laptop or handheld device can be found at www.bryantpark.org/amenities/wireless.php.

USEFUL WEBSITES

The **Lonely Planet** website (www.lonelyplanet.com) offers New York City information and links. Other good sites include:
New York City Search (www.newyork.citysearch.com)
New York Times (www.nytimes.com)
NYC & Co (www.nycvisit.com)
New York City Insider (www.theinsider.com)

Lost Property

Public transit (☎ 212-712-4500)
Taxi (☎ 212-692-8294)

Money
CURRENCY
The monetary unit used is the US dollar, which is divided into 100 cents (¢). Coins come in 1¢ (penny), 5¢ (nickel), 10¢ (dime), 25¢ (quarter), 50¢ (half-dollar; rare) and $1 denominations. Notes come in $1, $2 (rare), $5, $10, $20, $50 and $100. Some shops won't accept notes higher than $20.

TRAVELER'S CHECKS
American Express (☎ 800-221-7282) and **Thomas Cook** (☎ 800-287-7362) traveler's checks are widely accepted and can be replaced if stolen or lost. Restaurants, hotels and most stores readily accept US-dollar traveler's checks. Fast food restaurants and smaller businesses may refuse to accept checks.

CREDIT CARDS
Visa, MasterCard (both affiliated with European Access Cards) and American Express are widely accepted, Discover and Diners Club less so. For lost cards, contact:

American Express (☎ 800-992-3404)

Diners Club (☎ 800-234-6377)

Discover (☎ 800-347-2683)

MasterCard (☎ 800-826-2181)

Visa (☎ 800-336-8472)

ATMS
You'll find 24-hour ATMs at banks and most grocery stores. If you use a machine outside your bank's system, the ATM owner is likely to charge a small fee.

CHANGING MONEY
Banks often do better deals than exchange offices, but it's always a good idea to check the rates, commissions and any other charges. Chase, a bank with 80 branches in Manhattan, has no fees. Several Chinatown banks along Canal St are open weekends.

Newspapers & Magazines
The *New York Times* is the nation's premier newspaper; its Weekend section, published Friday, is invaluable guide to cultural events. The weekly *New York Observer* specializes in local media and politics. The *Daily News* and *New York Post* are popular tabloids. The *Wall Street Journal* is the daily business bible.

Time Out New York lists events, restaurants and shops; the *New Yorker* magazine covers high-brow theater, art and music events. Free street papers – such as the *Village Voice* and *New York Press* – offer good entertainment listings.

Photography & Video
Luggage is usually subject to high impact X-rays at airports, so pack your film in your carry-on bag. Print film is widely available at supermarkets and discount drugstores; 35mm slide film is harder to find. Camera shops stock B&W film. If you purchase a video, note that the USA uses NTSC color TV standard, which is not compatible with the other standards (PAL or SECAM) used elsewhere.

Post
OPENING HOURS
The main **post office** (3, B2; ☎ 212-967-8585; 421 Eighth Ave at 33rd St) is open 24 hours. The **Rockefeller Center post office** (2, C8) is open Monday to Friday 9:30am to 5:30pm. The **Franklin D Roosevelt post office** (2, D7; 909 Third Ave) is open Monday to Friday 9am to 8pm and Saturday 10am to 2pm.

POSTAL RATES
Domestic/international rates are: 37¢/63¢ for letters, 21¢/75¢ for postcards. Stamps are available from post office counters and vending machines. Buying them

from hotel concierges and souvenir stores costs 25% more.

Radio

Among the more than 50 radio stations, WBAI (99.5FM) is an interesting independent station; WINS (1010AM) offers continuous news and weather; WNYC (880AM) is the New York branch of the excellent National Public Radio network. WNYU (89.1FM) is the local college station.

Telephone

Public phones are either coin- or card-operated; some accept credit cards. Bell Atlantic phones are the most reliable. Use a major carrier such as **AT&T** (☎ 800-321-0288) for long distance calls.

PHONE CARDS

Newsstands and pharmacies sell prepaid phone cards but they can be huge rip-offs, charging per-minute prices a lot higher than those promised.

MOBILE PHONES

The US uses the GSM system – you'll need a GSM compatible phone to make and receive calls.

COUNTRY & CITY AREA CODES

The US country code is 1. Manhattan phone numbers are always preceded by a three-digit area code: ☎ 212, ☎ 646, and ☎ 917, although ☎ 646 and ☎ 917 also do double duty as mobile phone and pager area codes. Even when dialing in Manhattan you must use 1 plus the entire 10-digit number. For the outer boroughs, the area codes are ☎ 718 and ☎ 347.

USEFUL NUMBERS

City information (☎ 311)
Directory assistance (☎ 411)
International dialing code (☎ 011)
Operator (☎ 0)

Operator-assisted calls (☎ 01 + the number; an operator will come on the line once you have dialed)
Collect calls (☎ 0)
Time (☎ 212-976-1616)
Weather (☎ 212-976-1212)
Moviefone (☎ 212-777-FILM)
Clubfone (☎ 212-777-CLUB)

INTERNATIONAL CODES

Dial ☎ 00 followed by the code for the country you're calling:
Australia (☎ 61)
Canada (☎ 1)
Japan (☎ 81)
New Zealand (☎ 64)
South Africa (☎ 27)
UK (☎ 44)

Television

The four major broadcast networks (NBC, CBS, ABC and FOX) offer familiar prime-time fare; alternatives are the local New York 1 and the Public Broadcasting Service (PBS). Well-known cable networks include CNN, MTV and HBO.

Time

New York is in the Eastern Standard Time (EST) zone, five hours behind Greenwich Mean Time (GMT). Daylight saving starts on the first Sunday in April (clocks are advanced an hour) and it finishes on the last Saturday in October.

At noon in New York it's 9am in San Francisco, 5pm in London, 6pm in Paris, 7pm in Cape Town and 3am the next day in Sydney.

Tipping

Waiters expect a tip of 15–20% of the total bill amount from satisfied customers. If you aren't satisfied, that's another story. Tips are not automatically included in bills (although some restaurants do add a 15% gratuity to parties of six or more), so if you leave without tipping, it's not unheard of for a manager to ask you what was wrong. As a general rule you do not have to tip on tax (8.625% in New York). For an easy way to figure out the correct amount to tip, look at the tax you've been assessed and double it.

Other standard tipping amounts include:

Baggage carriers $1 for the first bag, 50¢ for each additional bag.

Bars At least $1 per drink (or more for faster service and stronger drinks).

Cloakroom attendants $1 per item.

Hotel service personnel $1 for each service performed.

Hairdressers 15%

Restaurants 15–20% (not expected in fast food, takeout or self-service restaurants).

Room cleaners Up to $5 per day.

Taxis 10–15%

Tour guides $10 per family/group for a full-day tour.

Toilets
Public toilets are rare, and commercial establishments provide facilities for customers only. If you're in distress, head to a department store or a fast-food restaurant.

Tourist Information
NYC & Co (2, C7; ☎ 212-484-1222; www.nycvisit.com; 810 Seventh Ave at 53rd St; ☽ 8:30am-6pm Mon-Fri & 9am-5pm Sat-Sun) operates a 24-hour toll-free line with listings of special events and reservation details. Staff are helpful and knowledgeable and the information center is comprehensive.

You'll also find information counters and centers at airports, in Times Sq (2, C8), at Grand Central Terminal (2, D8) and Penn Station (3, B2). The **Big Apple Greeters Program** (☎ 212-669-8159; www .bigapplegreeter.org; 1 Centre St) organizes volunteers to introduce visitors to the city for free.

For other sources of information, see p120 and p119.

Women Travelers
Women need not be too concerned about traveling on their own in New York City. Many shun the subways, but in reality the transit system boasts a lower crime rate than the streets. At night, you might consider riding in the conductor's car (in the middle of the train) and try to get in cars that have a few other riders inside.

Tampons and pads are widely available, though there's a smaller selection of tampons in the US than in Europe or Australia. The contraceptive pill and 'morning after' pill are available by prescription only. New York City law stipulates that rape victims be offered the 'morning after' pill while receiving treatment at hospitals, but it's not always automatically offered. If you want to take it, insist upon getting it.

LANGUAGE
New Yorkers speak the standard American idiom with a few special twists. Countless words borrowed from the languages of successive waves of immigrants have added extra depth to local expressions, so 'Forget about it' becomes 'Fuggedaboutit' – said with the appropriate Italian flair. 'Mazel tov' ('Congratulations') is used by all and 'Oy!' is often heard in moments of stress. Spanish has become the de facto second language of the city (sometimes called Spanglish), and *bodega* (corner deli), *hola* (hello), *adios* (goodbye), *hasta la vista* (see you) and *cerveza* (beer) are all part of the lingua franca.

Index

See also separate indexes for Eating (p125), Sleeping (p126), Shopping (p126) and Sights with map references (p127).

EATING

SLEEPING

SHOPPING

Sights Index

FEATURES

🏨 Comfort Diner .... *Eating*
🎭 Majestic Theater .... *Entertainment*
🍷 Bemelman's Bar .... *Drinking*
🏛 Statue of Liberty .... *Highlights*
🏬 Bloomingdale's .... *Shopping*
🏛 Skyscraper Museum .... *Sights/Activities*
🛏 Four Seasons .... *Sleeping*

AREAS

.... Building
.... Land
.... Mall
.... Other Area
.... Park/Cemetery
.... Sports
.... Urban

HYDROGRAPHY

.... River, Creek
.... Water

BOUNDARIES

.... State, Provincial
.... Regional, Suburb
.... International

ROUTES

.... Tollway
.... Freeway
.... Primary Road
.... Secondary Road
.... Tertiary Road
.... Lane
.... Under Construction
.... One-Way Street
.... Unsealed Road
.... Mall/Steps
.... Tunnel
.... Walking Path
.... Walking Trail/Track
.... Walking Tour

TRANSPORT

.... Airport, Airfield
.... Bus Route
.... Ferry
.... General Transport
.... Subway Station
.... Rail

SYMBOLS

🏧 .... Bank, ATM
🕊 .... Buddhist
✝ .... Christian
🏛 .... Embassy, Consulate
✚ .... Hospital, Clinic
❓ .... Information
@ .... Internet Access
☪ .... Islamic
✡ .... Jewish
🏛 .... Monument
🌳 .... Park
🅿 .... Parking Area
● .... Point of Interest
👮 .... Police Station
✉ .... Post Office
🚻 .... Toilets
🐾 .... Zoo, Bird Sanctuary

24/7 travel advice
www.lonelyplanet.com